OBSERVATIONS OF AMERICA AND MY ANCESTRAL PAST

OBSERVATIONS OF AMERICA AND MY ANCESTRAL PAST

An Epistolary Autobiography

RICHARD P. SINAY

To My Wife, Tina,
for her unwavering love and support for my writing.

To My Brother, Gary,
for encouraging me to take the trip without him.

TABLE OF CONTENTS

"A House Divided Against Itself Cannot Stand."

−ABRAHAM LINCOLN

PREFACE

When there is only one life to live and making a living is a good part of it, there is only a little time to complete the bucket list that most people have in the back of their minds. I remember in high school, a person named John Goddard used to come to our high school and show films of his adventures. He would narrate the adventure as the movie ran, and we sat amazed at his daring adventures. He had made a list of 127 life goals before he passed away. He finished 109 of those goals before he died in 2013 at ninety. Anyone can look him up on the internet and view what he managed to accomplish. My experiences pale by comparison, but the idea was the same. I had my set of preferences to achieve, and so did he.

One of those preferences was to set out and see as much of our country as possible and knock off a few of those bucket list items. With the encouragement of my brother Gary, who I wanted to go with me but couldn't, I set out in early May of 2014 to accomplish some of those goals. I also wanted to research my ancestry because there was some mystery about the exact origin of my paternal grandfather and grandmother. After the research, I wanted to share the findings with many of my first cousins on my father's side to dispel all the rumors about their mysterious past. So I bought a new car, called it Rocinante, the name of Don Quixote's horse, and the same name one of my favorite authors, John Steinbeck, gave to his GMC truck that he drove around the country and documented in the book *Travels with Charley*. I did not have a dog with me, but I did have my golf clubs with me.

Initially, I had written the book as a blog on Facebook while I traveled and entertained all my Facebook friends with my adventures. I included pictures of my travels and my narration on Facebook to give my readers a vicarious experience. I have them. When I took the writings from all of my travels, it appeared that I had myself a book-length document.

Some liberties were taken in the book's production because these travels occurred in different years. I combined some of my other adventures into this book for the sake of garnering all those travels I did after I retired. I was inspired to write the book when I learned that a diary is a kind of autobiography called an Epistolary Autobiography. This is a small window into what I did with my life. My life is undoubtedly less accomplished than John Goddard's, but it was all I could do in the time that I had.

INTRODUCTION

America is the promised land, a paradise for many seeking asylum, a land sought by pilgrims from England looking for religious freedom. Our history is well known, and it has been a sordid one. This writing is not about the history of our country but about observations I made on an ancestry trip around the country. I traveled over twenty-five thousand miles across the country. My trip was designed to meet some of the 31 (two had already passed away) first cousins I have on my father's side and 14 (two had passed away) first cousins on my mother's side. I had ancestry.com research the origins of my grandparents on both sides of my family. What was discovered was different than anyone had known before, and I wanted to share the new findings. Those findings are in the back of the book as Appendix A and Appendix B. The intent is to share with future generations the origins of their ancestors. In addition to that goal, I wanted to check off some of my bucket list items, visit the homes of literary writers I had taught for thirty-seven years, visit important American history sights I had also taught, visit our Nation's capital in Washington D.C., and see the topography of the country.

During my trip, I discovered an America I realized was different than I thought. I detail those differences in my comments on the day-to-day travels I made. Although this is not John Steinbeck's <u>Travels with Charley</u> or William Least Heat-Moon's <u>Blue Highways</u>, this is my literary, historical, and bucket list journey across the country, sharing the news of my name with any of my first cousins willing to listen, discovering more about my past and America's past. I took this trip to spread the truth to two families with myths and misunderstandings about our grandparents. I discovered much about human nature and how people vary in their desire to know more about their ancestral past. While some shared my enthusiasm for knowing much about our ancestral past, others could not be bothered. Those who cared or didn't care ran across generational lines.

My trip was not only an opportunity to share my news with cousins; it was an opportunity for me to check off some of my bucket list items. I wanted to see as much of our country as I could. My trip was about taking stock of the country and visiting states I had never touched. I wanted to venture deep into our country's past, look at our beginnings and our foundation, and determine how the experiment of America has worked for the past two hundred and thirty-five years when our country won the Revolutionary War with Britain. My trip will take me to the first successful English settlement in America: Jamestown. My trip will also seek out the people of the Mayflower Compact and those settlers who came to find religious freedom. Then, there was time to explore the Revolutionary War and how the American Colonists fought for independence from Britain. There was also time to take a closer look at some of the prominent founding fathers of our country: George Washington, Thomas Jefferson, and James Madison. My adventures would take me to places where the American Civil War was fought and its impact on our society to the current day. I also managed to see several of the war memorials we have for those brave soldiers who fought in World War II, the Korean War, the Vietnam War, and others.

I went to see the homes of several of my favorite authors around the country. The houses of Ernest Hemingway, Jack London, Nathaniel Hawthorne, Herman Melville, Edith Wharton, Pearl Buck, Mark Twain, Henry David Thoreau, Ralph Waldo Emerson,

Emily Dickinson, and Loisa May Alcott, among others. Because they were authors I taught in American Literature during my long teaching career, I wanted to feel the ground they dwelt on, breathe the air they breathed, and take in the ambiance of their environments. Once, during the trip, I came across a path in the back of the home of Robert Frost that split and went two ways, and I thought, "This might have been the reason he wrote 'The Road Not Taken.' Then, I discovered that the poem was not written at that house but rather at another. I walked the gardens of Henry David Thoreau, who built them for the Emerson's, the Hawthorne's (it was a wedding gift), and the Alcotts. Mostly, I wanted to see the childhood home of Mark Twain and his resting place in Elmira, New York. I loved his wit and humor and would have been a Twain scholar if I had life to do all over again.

My trip would also take me to those places I had always dreamed of seeing: The Grand Canyon, New Orleans, Mount Rushmore, Old Faithful at Yellowstone National Park, Michigan Stadium, and several significant golf courses around the country that I wanted to play just once: Harbor Town Links, TPC Sawgrass, Oakland Hills Country Club, and several more. I also want to see the house where I grew up and the town where I lived as a child. I wanted to go home again, and I did the best I could.

Perhaps the most critical part of the trip was to visit and talk with as many of my first cousins on my mother and father's side. I wanted them to know about the true origin of their grandfathers and grandmothers. So I sought out as many of them as I could and as many of them who would see me. It was an effort to put to rest for once the origin of my name since I had spent my entire teaching career telling my students that my name was Czechoslovakian. Ironically, my name is Hungarian, but my ethnicity is Slovakian. I am a second-generation full Slovak. The Hungarians, who ruled the Austro-Hungarian Empire for fifty years, made everyone take Hungarian names. All four of my grandparents were born in Slovakia, and my parents were Slovaks. When I went to my old neighborhood, I saw The Slovak Club, a building in complete disarray. Perhaps ethnicity is not as important today as it was in the 1950s. Times have changed.

The trip was vital for me on many levels, and I want to share my observations of different things I discovered about America on this trip. I will share those observations at different times and when the situation mandates it. I have taught America's literature and history; it was time to see it firsthand. This is the day-to-day story of my trip, which started in early May 2014 and ended in mid-November.

PART 1

INDIO, CALIFORNIA TO NEW ORLEANS, LOUISIANA

"Travel is fatal to prejudice, bigotry, and narrow-mindedness, and many of our people need it sorely on these accounts. Broad, wholesome, charitable views of men and things cannot be acquired by vegetating in one little corner of the earth all one's lifetime."

–MARK TWAIN

MAY 3, 2014

I left Indio, California, at seven-thirty and drove to Apache Junction, Arizona. I have some high school friends in Apache Junction, so I decided to catch up with them on my way to Albuquerque, New Mexico, to meet the first of my cousins, Carol Mikusa L'Esperance. Today was a trip through the desert, through Blythe, a city of 22,000 people who live in the middle of the desert. Along the way, I noticed that the topography was almost lunar, showing how barren our planet can be. We live on planet Earth. We are just one tiny planet in a universe too vast to understand. What are we doing here? When I looked at the topography, it made me realize that we live on a planet in the Milky Way Galaxy, ninety-three million miles away from the nearest star, our sun. That, by itself, is a miracle since recent discoveries have determined that although there may be many Earth-like planets in our galaxy, they are not as plentiful as the number of stars and planets too far from their suns to foster life.

It almost seems that when one travels, the same fast food businesses can be found nationwide: the usual fast food places: McDonald's, Burger King, and Dairy Queen. As a nation, we are fat because we have all these fast food places. I assume I will eat from them throughout my long trip. I have no choice. I am in a hurry. Now, these fast food places expect people to be there for lunch. Sadly, there are no better choices. I am not meeting any cousins here, even though one resides just a few miles from Chandler, Arizona.

I don't know what keeps one from responding to a first cousin. It may be understandable that I have not seen this particular cousin in fifty years. That has a lot to do with it. I would understand a rejection of "Sorry, but we have other obligations now and cannot entertain." But the silence from this cousin is mysterious, and the total lack of a response is bizarre. The lack of a response indicates they just want to be left alone in their unit. I emailed a brother of this particular cousin, and he indicated that he did not even get a response from them. So I know it is not my silly desire to connect with cousins I have not seen in fifty years and talk about the family name and other things. So I gave up trying, and my first attempt to see a cousin failed. It is hard to imagine how one cannot even reply to a phone call or an email. There is something deeply troubling about that. I think I will learn why eventually. Along the way, one learns that members of families are estranged from their parents and siblings. At the time of this trip, only one uncle was left on both sides of my family. There are only first cousins, some of whom are beginning to pass away.

There is disagreement in every family. There are troubles in every family. Each of the ten families on my father's side had issues during their day. Then, the first cousins, all members of the Baby

Boom Generation, had their own families. Each has had its share of health-related troubles, sibling rivalry, or divorce. Each had their troubles. In my father's family, all members of the Greatest Generation, there were ten kids, and each of the ten kids got married and brought in a spouse to the mix of those ten children. Most of the spouses managed to work into the family well, and others did not. When the ten children of my father's family got married, one of the issues that made it difficult was that some of the ten children did not marry Catholics. My grandfather and grandmother were Catholic---very Catholic. They did not approve of those children who did not marry Catholics because they were from the "old country" (Slovakia), and the grandparents did not think of marrying out of their faith. Part of this journey is to learn how problematic that was for some of them and how they remedied it. Did they stay Catholic, or did they turn to another religion? If anything caused a rift in the family during my father's Silent Generation, it was marrying outside of the religion. One of my uncles left the state and moved to California to escape the stigma of marrying a protestant. It was tabu in my father's generation. It was not in the Baby Boomer generation.

I spent the night in a cheap motel in Apache Junction and waited to visit a Facebook friend whose husband was a fellow high school graduate.

MAY 4. 2014

Today was spent visiting the local cultural findings near Apache Junction. Apache Junction is located about 2600 feet above sea level at the base of Superstition Mountain. Superstition Mountain is famous for the treasure supposedly buried in the Lost Dutchman mine. Jacob Waltz was the lost Dutchman who claimed gold was buried in that mine. I visited the Superstition Mountain Museum, and there were artifacts related to the famous mountain. People have become enamored with this mountain, and many have given their lives looking for this mysterious treasure that never existed. Only recently, three young men from out of the state came to look for the treasure and only met with the loss of their lives. They found them all dead several miles away from anywhere safe in the mountains. It has claimed many lives.

After visiting the museum, which also had a small church and barn used in movies that Elvis Presley made with many other stars, the last movie Presley made was called "Charro," and it was the only one where he did not sing. I then drove to a Ghost town up the Goldfield road, where people resided during the gold rush. It was a charming town, just like a Western town would look in the movies. There, I saw the famed list of those people who tried to find the lost treasure. The list was long and deadly.

I also discovered a Southwest American artist named De Grazia, whose works have become very popular in the Southwest. I learned that one of the restaurants there was quite lovely, and I will return to it the next time I return. After that, I went to one of the lakes in the mountains called Canyon Lake. It was rather beautiful, and once I saw it, I returned to the motel.

I then spent the afternoon and evening with Owen and Melinda Larsen. Both were wonderful to talk to, and we enjoyed long conversations about everything we could think of. We talked politics, religion, and about La Habra High School in La Habra, California, where Owen and I had gone. I found them to be excellent conversationalists and enjoyed their company tremendously. I had a wonderful dinner there and left in the early evening. Other La Habra fellows were supposed to be there, but my last-minute change of plans caused them to alter their plans. Owen and Melinda Larsen were great to talk to. It was a wonderful day. Conversations go a lot better when there is a little wine involved and when the people share the same beliefs or background. We shared our knowledge of our classmates and what we understood about their lives.

MAY 5, 2014

I drove from Apache Junction to Sedona, AZ, and got out downtown to see what the town was like. It was a tourist town, but it was in a gorgeous area. The temperature was very nice because Sedona is about 4000 feet up. Sedona is so much different than other parts of Arizona. So much of Arizona is desert, and I don't care for it. However, the beauty of the Sedona desert is like no other. The incredible rock formations are worth the visit all by itself. The geographic surroundings of that desert inspired the artist colony of Sedona—just incredible beauty.

After Sedona, I went to the Grand Canyon and spent the day looking at this unbelievable geologic wonder. Even after looking at all the pictures in the world, one cannot imagine how stunning the views are of this Grand Canyon. It is a formation that took millions of years to achieve. When we think about our presence on the earth, Man has not been here all that long. If the Earth is 4.5 billion years old, man has not been here for an hour.

When I was walking along the Canyon, I was amazed by the stupid behavior of people who walked out near the edge of the canyon and peered over. Some people were not even stable walkers but ventured out just to get a picture. I took several pictures of these fools walking out on these ledges and wondered why they would not value their lives enough to take such a chance. Is life that meaningless, and is it so cheap that one can take a risk like that and think nothing of it? Every year, people end up falling off the edges of the Grand Canyon, all for the sacred picture of the Canyon in the background. I had a picture taken of me, but I was safely holding onto a railing while standing near the edge. It turned out just fine and is all the memory one needs. It is sad to learn of those who fall, thinking it is a horrible way to die.

GRAND CANYON

One can take a helicopter flight over the canyon, go rafting down the Colorado, or take a mule ride; it did not seem like I could handle something like that. Having spent five hours looking at this unreal geologic wonder, I had seen all the Grand Canyon I wanted. I returned to the hotel, wondering how long it took to form.

MAY 6, 2014

I drove to Albuquerque, New Mexico, from the Grand Canyon, and it was a long and challenging drive. I arrived at Bill and Carol Mikusa L'Esperance's house in the early afternoon. She was one of the children of my aunt, Margaret Sinay Mikusa. Her father, John, was the last aunt or uncle alive. We soon embarked on a ride to Old

Town Albuquerque. It was a charming little town within the town of Albuquerque. There was some stunningly beautiful pottery and gorgeous jewelry made by hand by various tribes of Indians in the town center. It wasn't cheap, though. All of the precious metals have increased in value.

After a visit to the town center, we went to take the longest tram ride in the country, but unfortunately, a motor was not operating correctly, so we did not go up. The ride takes one to the top of the mountain and gives one a view of the entire valley. Instead, Carol and I went to the restaurant to talk and wait for her husband, Bill, to join us for dinner. Carol spoke of her family, and I discovered what a charming person she was. She found herself asking questions about all of the other cousins. I gave her a breakdown of what I knew and went into depth about my family. Bill came to join us for dinner, and we had a wonderful time eating delicious Mexican food.

OLD TOWN ALBUQUERQUE

After dinner, we returned to the house, and I sat and talked with Carol for the rest of the evening. We took a trip into the past and discussed all we could remember about Ohio. I learned that her mother, Margaret, passed away at age fifty. She left seven children, and Margaret was the oldest. This was the first time I learned that cancer was a killer on my father's side of the family. Knowing one's family medical history is important because a doctor is more likely to diagnose a patient knowing the family history of illness. I believe that genetics is a strong dictator of one's life.

MAY 7, 2014

I visited Loveland, Colorado, to see Monica David Turner the following day. She was the daughter of my aunt Patricia Sinay David. I also met for the first time her husband, Will Turner. They were both just wonderful people. I had the best time with them. We started talking when I got there in the afternoon, around four o'clock, and talked the entire night. It was interesting to learn Monica's perspective of the family, and it was fun for her to learn how the other families were doing. What we did a lot was laugh. It was a lot of laughing. It is family trait of the Sinay's—they love to laugh. I learned that my dad used to call Monica "Monicaca" (Perhaps because she had poo in her diaper). Monica said that my dad would get a laugh from the other aunts and uncles when he said this "term of endearment."

I learned that Monica and others had worked for Grandma Sinay at her house and learned to improve her work ethic and earn some money. Monica and Judy Sinay used to work cleaning grandma's house when they were teenagers. It was a lesson that many of us got from grandma and grandpa. Do some work for me, and I will pay you. It was a lesson that many of the grandchildren undoubtedly got, and it was a "gift" that grandma and grandpa gave to their grandchildren.

I told Monica I cut the grass for Grandpa Sinay as a kid. I had to trim the grass along the sidewalk, and it had to be perfect because that is what Grandpa expected for the twenty-five cents he paid for my brother and me to do it. In the 1950s, children lived near their parents, and the grandkids saw their grandparents reasonably often. What I learned from Grandpa Sinay became invaluable in my life: When one does a job, do it well. I always made sure the grass in front of my house was well-manicured.

Monica and I talked about teaching and shared a commonality of teaching English. Her favorite author was Stephen King, which became a source of amusement for the rest of the time. Talking to her about the difference between a literary writer and a famous writer was hilarious. Monica felt that Stephen King was a great literary writer. I argued that he was a famous writer who found a formula for excellent horror storytelling and sold millions, scaring people.

Monica and Will Turner were just delightful people. What a gorgeous home they have in a lovely neighborhood in Loveland, Colorado. We had a lot of nice laughs. I loved the decorating taste Monica had in her house. It was like a professional decorator had arranged the design of the house.

MAY 8, 2014

I drove to Louisville, Colorado, and spent some time with my sweetheart Nancy DeVogel's son, Steve DeVogel, and his girlfriend, Amanda Leon. Steve and I got blasted at the bar, waiting for Amanda to come to dinner. We talked about a lot of subjects, and religion was among them. We talked about family and the characteristics of family. I told him our family's story and its name's origin. He was a good listener, and I enjoyed his company while we waited for Amanda. When Amanda arrived, I told a shortened version of my family history story. I learned that Amanda was fifty percent Slovak, so we bonded with that. She was born in the same region of Pennsylvania as my dad. We had a wonderful dinner of pizza, a salad and beer. I saw their house after dinner and found it very cute. They had done a lot of work on it. It was a lovely evening, and it was great to see them.

I also took a ride to the Coors Brewery in Golden, Colorado. It was exciting but so much like other brewery experiences. Coors beer was exciting when I first started drinking, but it doesn't do anything for me anymore. Pretty good water, though.

MAY 9, 2014

I left early in the morning for Taos, New Mexico, about a six-hour drive. It was all I wanted to do for a day, and driving for 8 hours was a bit too dangerous because I got tired. I took Highway 64 off of the I-25, and it was a beautiful ride. I finally got to Taos early afternoon, had lunch, and saw the artist's work in town. The artwork was fabulous, and seeing and talking to three artists in the local region was unreal. I wished I had the budget to buy the stuff that I liked. One or two artists were so unique that I wanted to buy their work. The artists that I talked to were so lovely and so accommodating. I took many pictures of the town, and it is very New Mexico with Pueblo-style buildings. Mostly, I love the area, which differs from other parts of New Mexico, like Santa Fe and Albuquerque. It was very relaxed today, and the cool air required a jacket. I am headed south tomorrow, so things should warm up a lot.

The main observation I made on my ride down here is the beauty of Colorado. It is a beautiful state. New Mexico is surprising in that it has a lot of variation depending on where one is in the state because it has a lot of diversity. I also have discovered that the people in New Mexico are amiable, and they have benefitted me along the way. When one visits these isolated parts of states, one learns there is a big disconnect between Washington, DC, and the general population who have to work and earn money no matter what Washington is doing (or not doing). From those who waited on me to gas station people to the artists in Taos, it was a wonderful experience to be in New Mexico. People are working and just trying to make a living wage and trying to get by in life. Washington does not affect them on a day-to-day basis.

MAY 10, 2014

I left Taos, New Mexico, early in the morning and drove to Amarillo, Texas. I took route 518 South and then 84 South to I-40 East. The trip along 518 was naturally beautiful and one of the prettiest settings I have ever seen. Driving through this area reminded me so much of what it is like driving through Europe, except for one huge thing: what Americans have done to dot the environment with a lot of trash. Old buildings, dilapidated residences, and cars strewn everywhere demonstrate the lack of respect for how we appear to the outside world. Not only was it unsightly, but it was embarrassing. Americans need to represent themselves better to the European visitor or to any visitor for that matter. Why is there such a plethora of dilapidated housing in those majestically beautiful areas? How does an area like that turn into a trailer home park? These Americans have no pride in where they live. There is no pride in what they own, and having the area strewn with trash does not bother them. Why is it that when we drive the country, we have to see a boneyard of cars everywhere? Why do we have to see abandoned houses that are not torn down? When I was in Ireland last year, I never saw anything like this. Why here? Can't we tear down our useless buildings under a federal requirement to keep the environment looking good? Can we not have car boneyards that blight the environment? How is it that this kind of trashing of the environment is not regulated?

In the same area, I could see many different Christian churches dotting the landscape. Is it Christian to live so carelessly? What does the Christian thing have to do with living like that? Does it have anything to do with it? Is it appropriate to live in such a different way than He intended? I just don't seem to get it. The main point is that this is not how we should represent ourselves in our country because we have so many people visiting from other countries; we should not have abandoned blighted areas. We should have more pride in how we represent how we live. Too many visitors are returning to their countries and saying what a bunch of slobs Americans are when they see the junked cars, run-down buildings, and general junk strewn in such a magnificent environment.

I crossed over into Texas and finally left New Mexico, and found it to be a lovely and divergent environment. The topography changed slightly when I got on I-40 East and drove through Texas. During my ride on I-40, there were a few moments when wind gusts moved the car sideways. If a significant gust of wind moves my car sideways, I can't imagine what a tornado's wind force would do. I arrived in Amarillo, Texas, at two in the afternoon and went to do the wash so I had clothes for New Orleans. I have one more long drive before the final stretch into New Orleans.

While driving across New Mexico and into Texas, I saw several veteran memorials in the little towns I encountered while traveling through New Mexico. Many of these towns have these memorials, but I noticed their size for such small towns. A small town giving up one of their sons or daughters was significant, but it was more than one. And they seemed to die in different wars and at different times. Is small-town America paying the price of our wars? Is recruitment easier there because these young people have nowhere to go and nothing to do living in a small town? I wondered.

MAY 11. 2014

Driving from Amarillo, Texas, to Fort Smith, Arkansas, was a straight shot but marked by high winds. I can understand when tornadoes come tearing up and down I 40 when I experienced the wind coming in for a storm. The wind tossed my car like a toy, and it was only a fifty mph wind with higher gusts. I stopped at a gas station outside of Oklahoma City, and a clerk indicated that a storm was coming, and the wind usually picks up with the approaching storm. She even indicated surprise at the strength of the winds. "We just don't know what is coming anymore," she uttered. Oklahomans just learn to take cover. It is as if the USA is under attack, and, indeed, it is. It is under attack by Mother Nature. She has been relentless in her attacks on the US. We are the recipients of these attacks by Nature because of our invention---the car. Indeed, it has been responsible for a lot of CO_2 emissions. So has the burning of coal. We have become victims of our emissions because Nature has been fighting back at being treated poorly over the last fifty years or so.

Strewn along the highway are the usual billboards that dot the landscape, making what might typically be a pretty view an ugly experience. I recall an advertiser putting up billboards to have people stop to buy food at his restaurant. Nowhere in Europe would a visitor find such advertising dotting the landscape along the roadways. We have cluttered the countryside with billboards that make the natural environment ugly. None of the highways of Europe would look like this; we are just too commercial.

Much of the advertising is for motorists to stop at our country's fast-food establishments. We are a fast-food nation with the same garbage food in every small and large town in America. Even in the smallest towns, one of these culprits sells fried food. It is another way that we have become victims of our environment. We have settled for fast food, and there is hardly a redeeming virtue in any of it. Morgan Spurlock's "Super Size Me" expose on McDonald's became a classic, but in the end, it had no impact on the company. Perhaps one can get a salad now at the restaurant, but many people don't go for the salads when those French Fries are beckoning. We blot the environment of our highways with billboards advertising fast food, and then we blot our bodies with it. It is a kind of sickness that Americans have.

So, this long trip focused on our need to change how we are treating our environment, and there is some hope. I saw two massive wind farms that were in Texas and Oklahoma. Both would reduce the emissions in the air. We need to move fast in that direction and start producing renewable energy. I thought of Boone Pickens and his desire to convert all cars and trucks to natural gas. If there is still time, we must move before it is too late. As for the problem of fast food, we need to turn to education and educate our kids about the problems with eating food at fast food restaurants. They are equally as damaging.

Finally, I thought of a perfect lesson plan as I listened to music from the '50s, '60s, '70s, '80s, and '90s. I thought it would be good to show students how connected poetry and music are and to show the connection through the lyrics of the songs and the content of certain poetry. Well, perhaps it is a project for my retirement. I need to keep busy!

MAY 12, 2014

I drove from Fort Smith, Arkansas, to New Orleans, Louisiana. That was about 583 miles and nearly 10 hours. I am glad I made the trip because it saved me a lot of time. I will not have an extensive drive like that for the rest of the trip. At least, I don't think so. Much of my trip on the road was marked by various incidents and observations.

Along I-40 in Arkansas, I saw a billboard sign that said, "If you die tonight, Heaven or Hell?" Then, below the quote was a phone number 1 800 The Truth. I was tempted to call and ask them what the truth was. How would they know if I was going to Heaven or Hell? The question is easy to answer if one just asks whether the whole concept of Heaven and Hell exists. Where is Heaven, and where is Hell? The universe is more vast and profound than any of us ever thought. How can we know where either place is if the universe is so vast?

As far as going to either one, Mark Twain has uttered, "I am indifferent to going to either Heaven or Hell since I have friends in both places." That whole question also brought to mind one of Hamlet's postulations in his "To be or not to be" speech. In that long rant, Hamlet poses the serious question of going to Heaven, and he wonders aloud if others who have discovered it have not come back to tell us of the joys, why should I want to go there early? The irony is that Hamlet does leave the earth by the end of the play. He got to go to the "undiscovered country from whose bourn (boundary) no man returns." Like Hamlet, it "puzzles the will." It kept me thinking.

Further down the road, I saw another sign before a Baptist Church that said, "Serve the Lord with Gladness." It was an odd expression that I would not assume anyone might make. Serve the Lord with Happiness, but not Gladness. I am glad that it is the end of the week, but I am happy that I am serving the Lord. It is just a grammar thing with me or more to the problem of correct usage. I noticed errors on signs everywhere. It seems English teachers have done some lousy teaching around these parts.

When I got to the north of Little Rock, Arkansas, I saw some of the community's destruction during the last set of tornadoes. It was unreal! It is not the same seeing it on TV as it is seeing it in person and realizing how devastating it is to the community and people's lives. The people who suffer from these devastating tornadoes have their worlds turned upside down. The state's people have come together and helped do a fundraiser for all those poor souls affected by these tornadoes. Aside from the terrible loss of fourteen lives, the destruction is something to see. It looks like a meat grinder went on a rampage and tore through things like they were nothing. Giant trees were snapped like twigs. This is another outcome of climate change and the destructive path that Nature has unleashed on the world. These natural disasters have happened in the past, but not with the regularity that they are happening now. They are scary and dangerous, and they won't be subsiding soon. One of the reasons I delayed getting here by a few days was that tornadoes were crashing through the area, and I did not want to get there in time to meet up with one. I am praying that we have no severe episodes again. I am watching the weather constantly. I managed to get down here in beautiful weather with very little rain. I am happy to be out of the tornado area for now.

During this trip, I have shared the road with many trucks and need to make a few observations about them. They are terrifying, and there are zillions of them. I am amazed at the number of them, and it is hard to understand how this country can operate without the hard work of these truck drivers. I am very impressed and amazed at how good these truck drivers are as drivers, and ninety-nine percent of them are pretty nice on the road. None of them has an attitude. They watch out for the small cars, and that includes me. There was only one episode where one came into my lane and nearly hit me, but it was not that close, and he had to invade my space because a car was on the side of the road. State laws require that they pull around the car that has stopped. So many exist: McDonald's, Wal-Mart, Target, and others. It is impressive how these trucks keep the country moving. It is a little-known fact that they keep the country supplied. Yet, they all burn diesel and spew too many pollutants into the air. I would like them converted to natural gas or become electric as soon as possible. Truck drivers are America's friends, but I assume it is a culture all by itself. I don't think I will join it for now. I think they keep the country supplied.

When I stopped for breakfast in Arkansas, I went into a shop attached to the gas station, and there were short-order cooks in there cooking up egg McMuffins, Arkansas style. I ordered two and was about to take them when the lady told her assistant, "We aren't cooking any more eggs today, honey." I said, "If you don't, you will have some unemployed chickens." She thought that was funny and laughed enough to reveal several missing teeth. She said, "Well, I'll cook 'em if they want 'em." I said, "Good, the chickens will be happy." And then I wished the ladies a fine day, and I went to eat my biscuit egg sandwich. They were nothing like McDonald's because they were ten times better. I liked her work much more, and I think the chickens were happy I spoke up for them.

In Transylvania, Louisiana, I saw another funny sign. It pointed the reader in the direction of the coffee house. The sign said, " Jehovah Java Gourmet Coffee House." Somehow, it struck me funny that one must invoke the good Lord while ordering coffee. Simply hilarious. But I assume it was an attractive name for a coffee house that would bring customers toting their Bibles. Come and drink your coffee, and we will talk about Jehovah. It just struck me as a bit funny.

While traveling through Louisiana, I saw a group of detainees working on the side of the road. The police officer in charge was on a horse, and the scene reminded me of the movie *Cool Hand Luke*. There is that scene in the movie when this rather endowed young lady washes her car, and the work crew starts making comments about the half-naked girl washing the car. It is a rather funny part of the movie. I was thinking of that as I drove by this work crew cutting grass on the side of the roads. The amount of grass on the sides of the roads was endless, so I thought of the endless task of Sisyphus. Sisyphus was a king of Ephyra (now known as Corinth) who was punished for chronic deceitfulness by being compelled to roll an immense boulder up a hill only to watch it roll back down the other side. Then, he was tasked to repeat this action forever. The state of Louisiana put these fellows in hard labor for their crimes. Is this not like slavery? Is this going to "reform" these fellows? Have they thought of maybe teaching them a skill? How about educating these fellows? Can they reform them, or will they live the fate of Sisyphus? For them, cutting grass on the side of the road is an endless task, especially in the heat and humidity of Arkansas.

The drive from Fort Smith, Arkansas, to New Orleans is beautiful. One is amazed at the farmland in Louisiana, Mississippi, and Arkansas. There are just miles and miles and miles of beautiful farmland. One can see that at one point in our history, these farmers needed help. That "help" led to a Civil War and the fight for the freedom of the "help." I will speak more of this when I visit the Civil War sites of Pennsylvania.

Driving into New Orleans is something one cannot forget, knowing that the highway that one drives into the city is elevated. No matter what direction one comes into New Orleans, it is on an elevated highway. New Orleans is below sea level, and getting to the land areas is difficult. When one finally does, it is like putting one's feet on the ground for the first time. The big Superdome is the first thing one sees on entering the city. Eventually, the driving takes one to the French Quarter, where all the interesting buildings are. I noticed that it is older than it appears on TV. It was much older than I thought, but some buildings have been beautifully kept. I arrived at Hotel Monteleone, and two guys came to take the stuff from my car to the garage. I had a "home" for three nights.

They took my car, parked it in the garage, and took my bags to the hotel. I left several pairs of sunglasses in the car, but I knew what was there, so I did not worry. If they disappear, I will get the hotel to pay for them. I was taken to my room on the seventh floor, and then I decided to go out and see the famous Bourbon Street.

This part of New Orleans is filled with alcohol joints and fraught with exciting characters. There are the shoeshine boys who want to "shine" your shoes for a "donation" and then try to intimidate you into giving them 20 bucks for a shoe shine that lasts 15 seconds. These guys want to rip you off for nothing. I gave the guy two bucks, and he felt insulted. I told him if he did not like it, let me show him the police officer looking at me down the street. Fortunately, there was a significant police presence on the streets, and it does not appear that too much could happen without them being there. I felt at least a bit safe in that situation, but too many of them gathered around me when it came to pay time for the shoeshine. I was worried that they would steal my wallet. I kept it tucked in my front pocket. It could have been worse, but I will make an issue of it because these guys are intimidating tourists out of their money. I do not think the city should allow them to intimidate tourists this way. It was ugly, and it was awkward.

Then there are the Pedicab bullshit guys who will take as much from you as you give them. I told one of them I would give him 20 bucks for a half-hour ride. I timed it, and he had to work for his money carrying my ass around the French Quarter, telling me silly stories about nothing. At least he was not intimidating. They should have to advertise their cost to the tourists. Some are charging whatever they want—another set of scam bags. They pretend to offer you something, but nothing is good about them.

The French Quarter is filled with bars serving Daiquiri's for nine dollars for a 12-ounce slushy drink. They are way too sweet, and they have too much alcohol. But it was a welcome pleasure after a long drive to get here. I could feel the effects of those drinks quickly, and I didn't care much about how sweet they were—not going to have any more of them.

Then, there are the tourist traps or little shops that sell tickets for "rides" around the city. It cost fifty dollars for a 2 hour ride around the city. I thought it was too expensive and unsure where it went. The workers did not do a hard sell as they do in New York or Philadelphia, and I never saw any of the big double buses running around the city like they would show us the highlights. One of the sales guys said there is much more here in New Orleans than in New York City. I thought about how limited their experience has been.

All along the street, some charlatans want you to go in and have a good time. One said she wouldn't "hurt me" if I came to her "room." I was not afraid of being hurt by her, but her pimp looked like an animal. And it would not be a fair deal when it came time to pay, so I told her, "Not tonight." She smiled at me, and the pimp was pissed. So far, New Orleans has not impressed me.

Then there is the jazz music being played in the park made famous by the jazz musicians of their day. Some of the groups that play are just okay and nothing special. They will pass the hat if you sit there enjoying the music. They do not pay for anything. Another guy passed a hat to the poor folk in New Orleans. And then some people just beg.

I was walking on the main street when a guy and his girlfriend asked me if I could give them some money for something to eat. I said, "You both look healthy, so get a job." What a crock. The place is filled with animals that want to take money out of your pocket. It is just a charlatan city—a bunch of beggars on the street who pretend to provide a service. And there are the palmists and the fortune tellers who apparently can tell you about your future. What a crock of bullshit that is. Another charlatan is selling nothing. I was disenchanted with my visit.

Then there was the good part: the food here is incredible. There are a lot of restaurants all over the place. It is hard to know what is good and what isn't, but I am told they would not be there very long if they were not good. There is a lot of competition for good eating here in New Orleans. I will be looking out for the charlatans tomorrow and watching to see if I can find my way to the more historical sites here in the French Quarter. Napoleon was supposed to stay here, and I am looking to see where that might be. Then, down at the hotel's entrance was a list of all the famous writers who had stayed at the Monteleone: Hemingway, Faulkner, and Fitzgerald, to name a few.

HOTEL MONTELEONE

MAY 13, 2014

This morning, I took the trolley down St. Charles Street to the end of the line and back and did people-watching the whole way. Besides seeing the neighborhoods of New Orleans, I watched many people get on and off the Trolley. A line segment was being redone, so we had to jump on a bus and take the bus to where the line started again. It was an experience and took about two and a half hours. There were some interesting things along the way.

The homes of New Orleans look very old, and the area looks run down and unattractive. While walking along St. Charles, I found the trees had grown to mammoth sizes, and many trees had lifted the sidewalks into cockeyed positions. There is no renewal in this city, and if there was, I did not see it. Most streets have houses that need to be taken care of or renewed. There are certainly examples of houses being renewed and revitalized, but, for the most part, they could be in better condition.

While riding on the Trolley, a woman decided to let out a volley of language that would embarrass the best of us. She was yelling these obscenities at the man sitting next to her, and I thought she was sitting next to her husband and letting him have it on the Trolley. But when I turned around to look at who it was, I saw a black woman sitting next to an older white man who looked utterly befuddled. She let him have it so bad that the Trolley operator had to tell her to calm down. I was surprised that the Trolley operator did not take action and usher her off the Trolley. It appeared to me that she just had a mental illness, but the anger she demonstrated in her voice was of such magnitude that I thought something deeper was going on. It was as if the black race was screaming obscenities at the white race for all the injustices suffered over the years in the South. Yesterday, when I picked up the newspaper, I saw an article about a black man who had spent over twenty years in jail for a crime he did not commit. I thought about the novel *To Kill a*

Mockingbird by Harper Lee and the injustice done to Tom Robinson, who is falsely accused of raping a white woman. I thought of Oprah Winfrey in the movie *The Color Purple,* where she had gone to vote and was required to guess how many jelly beans were in the jar so she could vote.

The "crazy" woman eventually got off the Trolley, and people watched her suspiciously as I talked to the man sitting beside her. He said he did not say anything to her. She just let loose with a horror of foul language. I said that I thought she had a mental illness, but I think her anger had deeper roots, but it is hard to know. I think we have these people running around in our society with mental illness, and there is no care for them. We have seen too many of these individuals take out their frustration on innocent victims in society. Unfortunately, no one is safe wherever they go in American Society: the movie theater, the grocery store, a school, a church, or a shopping mall are places people have lost their lives to those mentally ill gun-toting crazies. Although this lady was angry, it is fortunate she did not possess a gun, or the whole Trolley might have suffered.

Later, I was walking down the street when a young couple in front of me was approached by an older black man begging on the street. Whatever they said to him was unpleasant because he screamed after them as they walked away. He appeared to be another person with some mental illness and could not cope with his life. People seem unsympathetic to these individuals, and our society is equally unsympathetic. We need mental health care facilities just like we have hospitals.

New Orleans is filled with beggars. Many of them are young people looking for a fast buck. I had one walking toward me, and he held up a sign saying, "Money for Gumbo? I'm hungry." I said to him, "Too bad." It may seem insensitive to you, but you might agree with my insensitivity when you see how young and physically capable he was. Have we taught the current generation, the Millennials, to beg on the streets? There were several beggars with dogs who were smoking cigarettes. The gull someone must have begging for money while smoking cigarettes. Beggars are all over the place, sitting on corners and panhandling. It reminded me of New York in the 1970s before they removed all these people from the New York Streets. It also reminded me of the Dickens novel *Oliver Twist*. New Orleans is filled with them. There are those you feel sorry for because you can see they have a mental illness. Perhaps these are just an indication of the underlying problems in our society. Or is it just that too many of these young people feel entitled to beg from society? Who knows? I know it is just disturbing.

New Orleans is like any other major city in the country, with crime, murders, and the general misbehavior of particular citizens. When one turns on the news in these cities, there are reports of robbing and murders. It does not matter what city one is in in America: turn on the news and listen to the crime. Disturbing things happen no matter where one is in this country. If we got all the news from every city in the country, we might think we live in a psychiatric hospital. Do we?

On a brighter note, I managed a round of golf at the TPC Club of Louisiana. This is where they play the professional tournament, The Zurich Classic, just held three weeks ago. The course was in magnificent condition, and I loved it. It was a Pete Dye (the architect) course, and as a general rule, I do not like his courses, but this one is spectacularly beautiful. I joined two young guys who were locals on the 8th hole, and we played the rest of the way together. What I liked about them was their manners. They knew I was older but were so respectful because they always called me "sir." This is the training that young people get in the South, and it does not matter who they encounter; they call me "sir." I liked the respect, and I liked the value that they have. They removed their hats when we finished the round and shook my hand. I was very impressed. They liked that I could handle the golf clubs and made a lot of good shots on the back nine. I was happy that the rain did not come and waited until the end of the round when it started to come down. I loved my round of golf at TPC Louisiana. These young men were not afraid of the alligators that came out of the water on the course, and they would run them back into the water with their golf carts. I would not get near those ugly-looking suckers and learned Louisiana had two million alligators.

I used my Google navigation to get me from the hotel to the golf course and back. It worked like a charm, and I am so impressed with the navigation system in my Google phone. It has served me very well on this trip. I have one more day in New Orleans tomorrow and plan to see more of the French Quarter. I will visit some of the art galleries as well.

MAY 14, 2014

My goal today was to see as much of the city of New Orleans as I could and learn about the history of it. I started with a walking tour of the French Quarter to gain a little perspective of this beautiful place. I learned that the French originally discovered it but found the area needing help to make anything of it, so they handed it over to the Spanish (Spain), who had the same trouble as the French. Eventually, the French would take it back and sell it to the United States over time for 50 million dollars. Then there was that war with the Bloody British, the Civil War, Reconstruction, and then, eventually, the place we know today.

New Orleans grows on you. I can see that happening as each day passes, and I eat another beignet. It has a liveliness to the city, and it is upbeat. The Hotel Monteleone is on Royal Street, just one street over from Bourbon Street, and both streets have their personalities. Bourbon Street is the irrational part of the self, the crazy street with booze flowing like mad on every corner, women hanging out in front of burlesque houses ready to demonstrate their wares if you look their way, Charlatans looking to read your palm, beggars by the dozen looking for a quick buck for a bowl of Gumbo, men soliciting passers-by to come into their joint to drink "Big ASS" beers that are two for one and even three for one, and shoe shine guys looking to cajole another customer into a tricked up shoe shine. It is a crazy place, as I have already demonstrated. But it grows on you.

On the other hand, Royal Street is the rational part of the mind with reason left in it. It is much calmer with Bob Dylan type of singers in many doorways singing for a buck from a passerby. There are shops and souvenir places, and there is serenity about it. It may be because this is where the police precinct is! The people on this street are the old folks and families who have come to New Orleans for a good time. No beggars are on this street, as the police will have nothing of them. However, I saw them do little about all the beggars on Bourbon Street. There is something pathetic about all of these beggars.

I thought of F. Scott Fitzgerald and what he championed in *The Great Gatsby*-- -that America was this idyllic place where all people could succeed and accomplish the American Dream if they just reached out and grabbed it. Instead, as Fitzgerald suggests, the dream is not a dream but a nightmare where we wake up to this vast wasteland and find ourselves struggling to stay alive, and we do it at whatever cost. People and beggars are all out there, just trying to make a buck and survive. My shoeshine guy is one example. He has few skills, several missing teeth, and no prospects for the future. So he hustles tourists by "shining" their shoes and making money that way. In some respects, I respect him because he is trying instead of holding a sign up in front of himself that says, "Feed me." Did we create a new, quiet generation with young, capable men on the streets panhandling because they can find no work?

The walking tour of New Orleans taught me the city's history and the area and how it came to be called The French Quarter. The French discovered the area and claimed it for France. They worked it, and eventually, they had enough of it and handed it over to the Spanish, who put their stamp on the area. The Spanish liked to paint their houses vibrant colors, and the French less so. Americans like white, so the influence of those times still stands today. The streets were all in French for a long time and then converted to English in the 19th century. Ironically, the hero of the War of 1812 in New Orleans, Andrew Jackson, had two successive terms and did not carry the state of Louisiana either time, even though they saw him as a hero. The entire French Quarter burned down in 1788 when a guy left his window open and, with his candles burning, let the drapes catch fire. The warning system for the fire was tamed by the fact that it was Good Friday, and apparently, the priests would not allow the bells to be rung to warn people of the approaching fire. So goes the story. Who knows what the truth is? What it did was burn down all those plantation types of shelters that dominated the area in that period. The building codes changed; the new houses were brick and mortar and wrought iron. This is the look we see today.

The tour guide was good but too detailed about the stories of the past. People just want simple things to attach themselves to, and she was too much of a history teacher who needed to gain more knowledge of the area and tended to over-explain the details of a history of one thing. She was from a 10th-generation New Orleans family. She was pretty nice, though. I enjoyed her jabber. I could teach her how to make that lesson of hers more effective. The teacher started coming out of me.

After the walking tour, I got on the hop-on/hop-off tour bus, rode around New Orleans, and saw the whole thing in perspective—the Lake Pontchartrain and the Mississippi River border the city. The River did not overflow in Katrina, but the canals did because they could not hold the water back, and the entire city was eighty percent underwater. It is already an island of sorts, and it just got inundated from all sides. There was nowhere for the water to go. It is complicated without seeing it, but it is pretty understandable when you see the city itself. I was more impressed with people's efforts to improve the city and redo some residential areas by redoing existing buildings. People want to live in the city, and new places are being redone every week for young people to move into and work here. There are good schools here in the city. I thought parts of New Orleans looked pretty shabby, and many of the mansions and big homes on St. Charles was in disrepair. It has had its hay day. The belief is that young people want to live and work in the city.

The gentleman who gave the tour on the hop-on/hop-off bus was too proud to see what was right in front of his face about his city. He defended it and did not look at it objectively because he grew up there and remembered it in a better period. He thought the Oak trees on St. Charles Street were magnificent, and I thought they were destructive, forcing up sidewalks so severely that one cannot walk down the street without falling over or tripping every five steps. It was different from my neighborhood. It is an exciting city with an entire history and a mixed culture. It has different classes of people, too. When I leave, I will miss it. I have enjoyed it and am so glad I made it a part of my trip. It is a place I have always wanted to see, and now I have memories of it for a long time.

PART 2

NEW ORLEANS, LOUISIANA TO AUGUSTA, GEORGIA

MAY 15, 2014

My travels today took me from New Orleans to St. Augustine, Florida. It was an eight-and-a-half-hour drive, but it was straightforward. I took Interstate 10 out of New Orleans and drove nearly the entire length of the Southern seaboard to I-95 south to St. Augustine. There was traffic when I got to Jacksonville. The traffic there was mild, and I never stopped on the road once. That is a long way without stopping on the road.

I am in St. Augustine for two reasons: to see the World Golf Hall of Fame and to play the TPC Players Course at Ponte Vedra Beach. The Golf Hall of Fame is supposed to be spectacular, so I made the trip to see it (and hopefully get inducted). The more important reason is to play the TPC course where the PGA Tour plays The Players Championship, the unofficial 5th major of the golfing world. The other major golf tournaments are The Masters, the US Open, the Open, and the PGA. They all carry a five-year exemptions on the PGA tour, so a player who wins one of them is exempt on the PGA Tour for five years. The Tournament Players Club Course is unique and not one that anyone can play daily. I am lucky to be able to play it.

Just before I got to Jacksonville, the first real rain of the trip hit me. There was some rain in New Orleans, but not enough to get me wet. However, as I made my way along I-10, a big black cloud hung over the freeway, pouring like I had never seen rain. The windshield wipers worked full-time and could not keep the water off the windshield. It was pouring buckets of water, lasting about two miles, so I had to slow down to about 35 miles per hour. Once I broke through the storm, it was a beautiful day the rest of the way. I was at the hotel less than an hour later. It is incredible how much water can come down at one time. On the news tonight, the indication was that there was a lot of rain in North and South Carolina. A big cold wind came from the Rockies, pushing itself along the South. It was in the 50s the entire way here until I got to Florida, and it was only 75. It is going to be a perfect day for golf tomorrow. No rain is predicted, and a cool 78 degrees. I was super excited.

There was little to report on coming to Florida as so much of the freeway had trees lining it on both sides, so it felt like I was in a tunnel all day. I listened to the radio and heard about my former hometown getting attacked by fires. Some of the fires are close to where I lived but in different neighborhoods. I hope my brother's house is okay. I talked with him this morning, and the fires are far away. So, it reminded me of man's two biggest enemies: fire and water. William Faulkner believed that both are terrible enemies of man. I left New Orleans, and they fear the water there, and I left Southern California, and they fear the fire there. For some reason, my thinking reminds me of Robert Frost's poem:

Fire and Ice

Some say the world will end in fire,
Others say it will be ice,
But what I've tasted of desire,
I hold with those who favor fire,
But if it had to perish twice, I think

> I know enough of hate that for destruction,
> Ice is also great and would suffice.

This is the classic difference of opinion about how the world will end. The religious people say it will end in fire—Armageddon. Scientific people say the world will end in an ice age brought on by global cooling. I am unsure how things will go for our great planet, but extreme weather makes us think that we are going to deal with fire and we are going to deal with water (melted ice). So Frost hit on a notion long before our time when we are competing against both every year.

MAY 16, 2014

Today was a golf day. I woke up to a beautiful morning and thoughts of golf. Golf has been an important part of my life. I was able to do a lot of bonding with my son when we played golf together. There were many joys, and there were disappointments, too. Golf has given my son an avenue to be better than me. I think parents all want their children to be better than them, and if they don't, they have a problem. If a parent graduated from college, they should want their kids to do so and perhaps graduate from a better college. I think that for a parent to improve the lot of their children, they must take risks. It is what my grandfather did when he came to America to seek a better life for his children, and it is what my father did when he moved the family to California so his kids could have a better life. I had the opportunity to help get my son to an outstanding college through golf.

I took a risk by prioritizing golf for my son and a scholarship to Stanford. An eventual job opportunity at Google was the reward for that risk of making golf a priority. I am glad about all the effort he and I made to accomplish that goal. He has a very secure future; that is what you want for your children. Because his work and children keep him busy, playing golf is difficult for him to do right now. Since I am retired, golf is the game I love to play for fun and some exercise and getting out and bonding with nature. I love to play because it is such a tough game, and I enjoy playing challenging courses.

Before playing today, I went to the World Golf Hall of Fame in St. Augustine, Florida. It was amazing to see the accomplishments of the great golfers in golf history. I spent three hours there looking at some of the trophies won by many of the greatest golfers ever. I was in awe of the accomplishments of quite a few golfers. These players are the best; gaining entrance into the Golf Hall of Fame is an incredible accomplishment. Each one of the inductees is a unique golfer.

WORLD GOLF HALL OF FAME

Golf is not an easy sport; it requires tremendous dedication and hours of practice to learn the skills to make that ball do what you want. I have heard stories of the hours of dedication that many great players have given to the game. It is a lot harder than one thinks. Most people need to realize the number of hours that it takes to be as good as the professional players are. So, it is easy to be in awe of players' accomplishments and the kind of dedication it took to be as good as they are.

Today, I decided to challenge myself and play at a golf course near here where the professionals play for The Players Club Championship. The payout for the winner of this tournament is a huge 1.8 million dollars for one single win! Many tournaments now have a payday of one million for the winner. It's pretty good pay for four days of work, but the work to win the tournaments is put in long before they play. The distances from which these players play today make being good all the more challenging. I played from a distance of 6400 yards today because that is all I can play at age sixty-five. The professionals play from 7400 yards and play what I call "A Man's Course." I shot an 87. I double-bogeyed the last two holes, the toughest on the golf course. The wind played a crucial role in making the shots difficult on the last two holes. The seventeenth hole is an island green, playing from 142 yards straight into a two-club wind. It required an excellent five-iron to get the ball there. I hit the ball far enough but missed the green to the right, and it went into the water. The second ball I managed to get on the green. I got it up and down on the hole for a five, a double bogey.

THE 17TH AT TPC SAWGRASS

Number eighteen is one of the most challenging holes in golf on the PGA tour. I missed my third shot and ended up in the rough; I did not get it up and down, so I took a six on the hole, another double bogey. When I finished the eighteen holes, I was exhausted. The management required that we not drive the carts on the fairways, so we had to walk to every ball we hit. It was very tough. The course was very tough, and it cost me four hundred and fifty dollars to play the course. It was a once-in-a-lifetime experience.

It was a great experience because I played with two charming people. They were Dave and Myrna Miller. They lived in Ponte Vedra Beach, and they were super friendly people. I had dinner with them after the round of golf, and it gave me an idea of what it would be like to live in Florida. They were retired but still relatively young. He sold a chemical business for a substantial amount of money. He bought my dinner. When we got to the parking lot and said goodbye, they entered a Bentley, and I drove off in my Honda CRV. The difference between the business world and being a teacher. I had a great day. I arrived home at nine o'clock, had a super day, and went straight to bed. I slept very well, dreaming of my round of golf.

MAY 17, 18, 2014

I needed to get to Orlando to meet my sweetheart, Nancy, to share some fun at Disney World. I drove to St. Augustine and went to the historical site where Ponce De Leon discovered Florida and where the first settlement occurred in America. St. Augustine was settled in 1585, nearly twenty or so years before the settlement of Jamestown in 1603. After visiting the town of St. Augustine in the morning, I drove down to Orlando, Florida, and went to the hotel where Nancy was checking in. I arrived at 1:45 and came out of the restroom at the hotel, and there she was. She was so happy to see me, and I was so happy to see her. We got in the car and went to EPCOT, one of the Disney amusement parks that was quite interesting. We kept a good pace on the first day and managed to go on several rides. The weather was spectacular, and the park was not super crowded, so we rode many EPCOT rides.

DISNEY WORLD EPCOT

What I did learn about this place called EPCOT was that it was so commercial. A shop of toys waits at the end of every single ride in EPCOT, or a shop of merchandise that Disney has ready for one to buy. I cannot imagine what they thought when they made this place other than how they could monetize it. Disney is a corporation, and it is all about the bottom line. How much money did we make today? People are not buying things at EPCOT, given that few have bags. I did not spend any money on things but spent plenty of money on food and drink. This little excursion was expensive and not for people with light wallets.

If we took the ride "Figment of the Imagination," the doll " Figment" was on sale at the end of the ride. On visitations to the World Showcase, there were items for sale from each country we visited. It seems to have been chiefly a commercial sale of items related to the country we just visited in the section of EPCOT called World Showcase. Disney made an effort to include many different countries to show the diversity of people on earth and to include them so people from those countries could enjoy their stay. I just think it was very, very commercial, and quite evident that it was commercial. Making money is the fundamental objective of the park. The food prices were set to make a profit as well, and of course, the admission price had just gone up to ninety-six dollars a day per person plus tax!! I was shocked by the price, but as Nancy said, "We have been there and done that. Never again will I be trampled on the space of Disney World. Not worth it." But we still had a wonderful time, as we always do when we are together.

MAY 19, 2014

I drove to Fort Lauderdale, Florida, and saw a cousin I had never met. He and his wife were just enjoyable people. I had a great time with them. I got there at 6 o'clock and left at 12:30 a.m. Talking to someone related to you and someone I had never met before was a hoot, but I learned a great deal about my Aunt Mary Sinay Oleno/ Shull. She married twice and had two boys with the first husband and one son with the second son. The second son's name was Terry Shull, and we had a wonderful time eating Chinese food and drinking beer. I did not have much chance to see Fort Lauderdale because it took so long to get there.

I have found that my cousins have different knowledges of the family and different histories of the family. The cousins had different experiences with the other cousins and their families. I found that since we were out on the West Coast, we only had a relationship with the West Coast cousins, and the rest of them became just a figment of our imagination. Many of the cousins have never met each other. This one in Fort Lauderdale was someone I had never met. My sister said she had met him, but he said he never met my sister and that she only talked to him on the phone. I learned that Terry was estranged from his two half brothers, and only once did the three of them meet. One of them, Pete Oleno, has already passed away. He had a brother named Tim, who has become one of my favorite cousins. What I learned was interesting: most cousins had good work ethics like their parents.

My dad and his nine brothers and sisters all had excellent work ethics. I learned what each of the aunts and uncles did for a living. They were all excellent workers. Each aunt and uncle had children who became cousins, and of the 39 cousins, many were outstanding workers, too. However, the children of our generation were not as hard at working as we were. In short, the children of the Baby Boomers and those of the Silent Generation were likely to have weaker work ethics. As generations pass, fewer take on the values of the previous generation.

Another of the exciting topics that we discussed was the problem of weather. If you live in Florida, you have the hurricanes to deal with. If you live in California, then there are earthquakes to deal with. The area of the country dealing with weather issues is the

Midwest. We talked about what was worse! Each area of the country has problems, but we decided that tornadoes and hurricanes are more problematic than earthquakes.

I learned a lot about many of the cousins from Terry and found that he had spent more time with a variety of them than I had. Going to California distanced us from the family, and we did not get to see many of the cousins over the years, and now it is to the point where the cousins are starting to pass away. I decided to become closer to these people before I passed away. It has been fun so far, and much is yet to come.

MAY 20, 2014

Today, I headed for Key West, Florida, to see Ernest Hemingway's house when he traveled to that part of the country to do his Marlin fishing. Hemingway was a great sportsman, hunting in Africa and parts of the Northern states in America, a bullfighting aficionado, and a boxing lover. He loved many sports and wrote the Bible of bullfighting called *Death in the Afternoon*. I imagined that he thought of writing The Old Man and the Sea while fighting Marlin off the coast of Key West. It was quite a drive, but it was worth it. I took a tour of the house and met all the cats he had from several generations. Hemingway was a cat lover. He worked at his house each morning for several hours, writing his books. Then, he would turn to play and drink.

One of the more humorous parts of visiting the mansion is seeing all the cats running outside the house. Many of them have six toes in their front paws, and this trait has been passed down to the succeeding cats for several generations now. The cats are friendly, and some are just aggressive. It was a fun part of seeing the mansion. The house is incredible but not overwhelming. Hemingway lived simply and lived with the basics. A pool in the side yard was highly unusual for the 1930s. It was built for 20,000 dollars and hundreds of hours of labor because the men had to dig the 60 by 24 vast pool out of coral, a complex process. It was also ten feet deep on one end and five feet deep on the other. His wife at the time was Pauline, who oversaw the construction and spent more money than Hemingway was happy about paying. He dropped a penny on the ground near the pool, claiming that this was all he had left after the construction, and he told Pauline she might as well have that, too! It is embedded in the concrete near the pool. That was the beginning of that pool's costs because filling it with eighty thousand gallons of water was a feat. It was in the 1940s that fresh water came to Key West, and the pool could be filled with fresh water. It was filled with seawater for a long time, and emptying and cleaning it had to happen regularly.

The house was filled with furniture brought from Europe and the trophies Hemingway shot and killed on his African safaris. I am unsure how to slay an elephant, but those were the times then. Hemingway wrote much of his adventure in Africa with his book *Green Hills of Africa*. This is the book where Hemingway claims that "all modern American Literature comes from one book by Mr. Mark Twain, *Huckleberry Finn*." The explanation for Hemingway saying this will come later in the book because I discuss this when I visit the houses of Mark Twain.

The grounds are filled with gorgeous flora that is tropical and beautiful. Since photographs were not permitted in the house, I did not think to take them outside, but one can see the beauty of the flora online. It was well worth the trip to visit Hemingway's house. I took a graduate seminar in Hemingway with one of my favorite professors, Dr. George Friend. During his class, I wrote a paper on *The Sun Also Rises* and argued that the characters in the novel were just going round and round in circles and going nowhere. I opened the paper with a quote from J. D. Salinger's novel *The Catcher in the Rye:*

"Then the carousel started, and I watched her go round and round...
All the kids tried to grab for the gold ring, and so was old Phoebe, and
I was sort of afraid she'd fall off the goddam horse, but I didn't say
or do anything. The thing with kids is, if they want to grab the gold
ring, you have to let them do it and not say anything. If they fall off,
they fall off, but it is bad to say anything to them." (Salinger 210)

When I finished reading this introductory quote, Dr. Friend said, "Stop right there. I know exactly what you are going to say in your paper. This is the kind of paper I have been looking for, folks. We have not had a paper like this yet. Mr. Sinay is going to argue that the characters in the novel spent their time going in circles and essentially going nowhere in life." George Friend was precisely correct. Then he let me read my paper, and I proved his analysis precisely correct. It was a seminal moment as a writer, and I felt I could manage any writing afterward.

I spent the night in Key West and dreamed of catching a big fish.

MAY 21, 2014

Today, I drove far from Key West to Savannah, Georgia. There's not much to say about my drive except that Florida is flat and has many palm trees. I visited two areas on the drive: Port Lucie and Port Orange. Port Orange is where Carol DeVogel Lockett, my sweetheart's daughter, wants to live in the not-too-distant future. I liked it, and I thought it was a lovely area. Sometimes, we will have to go down there and look at ourselves. The hurricanes of Florida are what makes it unattractive to live in. I cannot see the benefit of living in such a turbulent environment. Sometimes, vacating the state is the only way to stay safe. I just can't imagine doing this from time to time. The I-95 is one of the most insane freeways I have ever driven. The traffic is mind-boggling, and this freeway has more accidents than most in the country. It is a dangerous freeway, and one I am glad is behind me.

I arrived at 6 o'clock and had some time to go to the historic district and have dinner. It was pretty nice. I had some Southern chicken wings. Tomorrow I am going to take a trip around the city and enjoy the history of the city.

MAY 22, 2014

I woke up in Savannah, Georgia, and spent the morning taking a city tour. The Savannah Tours takes people around the Savannah Historic District, and they tell the same stories repeatedly. I am sure the trolley driver is tired of repeatedly hearing the tour person say the same thing. She was a real Southern lady with all the accompanying biases. During the tour, she called the Civil War "The War of Northern Aggression." I found this hilarious with people who still have a bias about the Civil War, and that if they did not want to give up Slavery, did they just want to perpetuate that forever? There was bitterness in her voice. Are Southerners still angry about the Civil War? I think so, and it tells vividly in our politics. A black man is president, and the white people are angry. Ironically, they don't see him as half-white, but they see him as all-black. In his speech on August 28, 1963, Martin Luther King's comment comes to mind: "I have a dream that my four children will one day live in a nation where they will not be judged by the color of their skin but by the content of their character."

I was not particularly pleased with her because she talked too fast and tried to be funny, but she wasn't. She even told a joke, and nobody laughed. There were plenty of Southerners on this ride. After a while, nobody would get off at any of the stops because we wanted to go the whole route before deciding what we wanted to see more of. So she stood at the front of the bus and pleaded with people to get off. Finally, she unloaded a boatload of people who were annoyed with her anyway. She gave too much information and did what I call information overload to the point where one needed to learn what she was talking about, so people started to talk and not listen to her. At the beginning of the ride, she asked if someone wanted to be the "slapper" or someone who would slap people if they started talking. I thought that was rude of her, to be honest with you. People would not start talking if you are interesting enough or can communicate effectively. She would see things ahead of her and talk about them, and the people could not see what she was talking about. Weird. I sat in the front and managed to see what she was talking about, so my position allowed me to see things. Anyway, I did not tip her. I got off and wandered the city for a couple of hours and found the city to be architecturally magnificent.

The famous James Oglethorpe did the layout of the city. He designed the city of Savannah and did some beautiful things. Many movies were made in Savannah, of which *Forest Gump i*s one of the most famous and *Midnight in the Garden of Good and Evil.* The bench Forest sat on is not there, but the location still is. The restaurant where Jennie, his love, worked is still there. There are many magnificent buildings, and one could spend a long time looking at them. I had to move on.

I drove to Hilton Head Island to see if I could play the Harbor Town Golf Links, one of the most famous golf courses in the country. The pros play a yearly tournament there. While driving there, I saw signs saying "Evacuation Route." I understood what this part of the country was going through when hurricanes came to town. They had to get out. I played the course from 6400 yards, with a slope of 137 from the back tees, which means the course is pretty challenging. The slope is the number attributed to the course to indicate the level of difficulty based on what objects are in the way of the golf course. Remember TPC at Sawgrass? That has a slope of 157 from the back tees! Extremely difficult.

HARBOUR TOWN GOLF LINKS

I played with two local guys who had played the course, according to Dropper, a thousand times! He and his partner, John, had a match, and I just asked them where to hit the ball. I did not hit the ball long, but I hit it straight and shot a good round of golf. At the beginning of the round, I said, "This cannot be as hard as TPC Sawgrass." They decided to "defend" Harbor Town by saying the underpar was less than TPC Sawgrass. It does not matter, I thought to myself. This course was more accessible because I killed it better than TPC Sawgrass. Sawgrass is a nightmare golf course!! When Tiger says it is hard, then it is hard!! More importantly, it is one of the most beautiful golf courses I have ever played, and I thoroughly enjoyed it! I think it is a natural beauty and a great design. I never hit a single tree all day, but the two I played with spent their lives in the trees. One must hit the ball straight here. They could not believe I was playing the course for the first time.

As to the beauty of the golf course, playing golf has the benefit of bonding with nature, or as Thoreau would put it, "suck out all the marrow" of nature while hitting a golf ball. One is free from care, responsibility, troubles, and bondage when playing on a beautiful golf course—there is more to golf than just hitting a ball with a crooked stick.

After the round, I bought the two locals a beer and chatted in the clubhouse. It was interesting to see their perspective of the area. Americans are so biased to their area, and most never travel outside of where they live; they become ensconced in their milieu and never break out of it. A sociological term exists for people who never venture out of their area. They were nice guys but a bit leery of people from California. I guess they think everyone from there is gay or crazy. They were excellent to play a round of golf with, but I am not sure I could handle their viewpoints for more than a couple of rounds of golf. Around the golf course were many homes, and they were beautiful. I like the Southern architectural home style; they build an esthetically pretty home.

I finished and then drove the two hours to Charleston, South Carolina; I got situated in the hotel and found a local dinner place. I ate some grits, hush puppies, and Salmon patties, and my stomach will never be the same. I had to let a few more inches of the pants out as I ate this meal! Ugh. I will have to starve tomorrow. I took the time to ask the waitress what each of the things was that I was eating. It was a hoot with the waitress saying, "You never had any grits?" Well, no, not like this! It was a good meal, and I am done with fattening foods from the South. Paula Dean can have it. There was too much grease and too many fried things. They know nothing but frying food.

I got back to the room and turned on the news, and a guy who killed another guy was being sentenced for killing him. Is this the same mantra I have heard in every other city on this trip? What is it that people grow up and never think that there will be consequences to doing something like killing someone? I guess the death penalty is no deterrent and has never been and never will be. People seem to get caught up in the heat of the moment when they decide to take another person's life. Are we animals or humans? One can be sure that the animal comes out of a person when they are passionate about hurting someone. I lived long enough to learn that people are sometimes killed in heinous ways. The death penalty is usually the court's response.

When I taught my argumentative research paper in high school and the freshman English classes at college, this topic was often discussed, and differing arguments would be made for both sides. Some of my students would argue vehemently about the necessity for capital punishment, and others would be less punitive and allow the culprit life in prison without parole. The sad thing is that God should not have made us want to kill each other. Whether killing is done on an individual level or in a war, why is man taking the lives of their fellow men? We all know that wars come to nothing but a lot of dead people. I was a pacifist when I was a freshman in college, and I am still a pacifist. I am not sure that man will survive with the proliferation of nuclear weapons. I hope I am not around to see it.

I was meeting a cousin about an hour away tomorrow, but he called me to tell me he is right here in Charleston, so I will see him tomorrow. I will see the city tomorrow, my cousin, and then I am off for a ride to Augusta, Georgia. I plan to see Augusta National Golf Club. I'm crossing my fingers.

MAY 23, 2014

Today, I got up to start the day touring the city of Charleston. I could not believe some of the gorgeous buildings that the city has and how pricey they can be. One of the mansions I saw was recently purchased for thirteen million dollars. There were so many beautiful homes in this area that I wanted to move here, but I did not think I could afford it.

When I went to take the tour of Charleston, I had called a cousin of mine to see if I could visit him about an hour or so north of Charleston, but it turned out that he and his wife were in Charleston with some friends! So I had lunch with Mike and Laura Labak, one of my first cousins on my mother's side. It just so happened that I had learned from my genealogist what my grandmother's maiden name was! Also, the names of my grandmother's mother and father! He was just thrilled to learn what their names were and where they were born. It turns out that they, like my father's parents, were also born in Slovakia. I learned today definitively that I am 100% Slovakian. Slovakia was formed in 1993 after being a part of the Czech Republic since WW I. So, as I go around the country and meet my cousins, I am still discovering who I am. It has been enormously gratifying. I can understand why I love Hungarian food at a restaurant in Pennsylvania called Paprika's. I'm looking forward to a few meals there this summer.

There is a vast disparity between the rich and the poor in Charleston. I see so many homes that look uninhabitable but are being lived in. I cannot get used to the idea that many people live in squalor. There needs to be a better way to even out the disparity. I spent little time in Charleston, South Carolina, but I had an excellent guide on the tour. He did it right, and he did it perfectly. He stopped at the houses and turned and talked to us and made it very personal. He showed us where the Civil War began at Fort Sumter and the engagement that went on for twenty-four hours before the Southerners took the military weapons facility from the federal troops and sent them packing.

I learned that South Carolina farmed cotton and rice before the Civil War and then lost both crops after the war was over. They needed the laborers to do the work. There was history after history of situations that made Southerners rich before the war, and then all was lost after the war. There was a lot of suffering, and it brings it home when one sees how everyone was affected. I felt the heat and humidity of the South for the first time today, and the weather got hot, and the humidity rose. Every part of the country has crosses to bear regarding weather. There is no place I know that is perfect, but maybe Maui is as close to perfect as possible. Many of us don't realize the daily work farmers put in to feed this country and the miles and miles of farmland that grow crops to feed us or the animals. Thank goodness for the farmers and all those who labor to have these things on the table daily. I am super excited about tomorrow and must turn in for the alarm to go off early.

I then drove from Charleston to Augusta, Georgia. I came to Augusta with a silly notion: I simply wanted to see the area surrounding the most revered golf course in the country, and that, of course, is Augusta National Golf Club. I drove around the golf course, but there was very little to see, so I was disappointed in how blocked the golf course is from public view. So I drove around Augusta and saw what I thought was a very ordinary town. It was nothing special and unquestionably not nearly as immaculate as the pristine fairways of Augusta National Golf Course. It is, of course, where they play the Masters every year, and it is one of the country's most sought-after rounds of golf. I kidded my brother, Gary, about meeting Jack Nicklaus and Arnold Palmer there for a round of golf, and I fantasized about the possibility of meeting someone who could let me play with them.

Well, I got half of my dream taken care of when I went to dinner. While eating at the bar at O'Donovan's (now Sheehan's) Irish Pub in town, I heard two guys talking about playing Augusta National. Their names were Mark Ritchie and Pat Becker. They were just giddy about their experience at Augusta National, and I kind of winked and nodded as they continued the conversation. After a short time, they invited me to their part of the bar, introduced themselves, and asked if I wanted to play Augusta Country Club the next day!

MARK RITCHIE AT AUGUSTA COUNTRY CLUB

I could not believe my ears, and before long, we exchanged numbers, and I am set to tee off with them at 8 a.m. tomorrow. I cannot believe my luck. Augusta Country Club is next door to Augusta National, and I will be able to see some of the holes of

Augusta National from my playing at the country club! This is so exciting. I cannot believe it. So I will write about my experience on that course tomorrow.

MAY 24, 2014

Today was a truly incredible and fortunate day for me. I got to play at Augusta Country Club in Augusta, Georgia. This is the sister course to Big Brother, Augusta National Golf Course, where they play the Masters. As I already indicated, I had dinner last night at an Irish Pub and met two wonderful guys from Chicago named Mark Ritchie and Pat Becker. We got along immediately and had a wonderful time drinking and talking golf. They both had just played Augusta National, and they were sky-high with excitement, so naturally, I wanted to hear about it. I patiently listened as they narrated their experience, and before long, they indicated they would play Augusta Country Club the next day, and I could join them. I was so excited that I must have thanked them a thousand times. I hope people always hear thank you.

We showed up at the course early and got set up to play. We were treated with dignity and respect. They treated us like members, and we played the 18 holes and then ate lunch in the men's grille room. We could not believe how extraordinary it was when we played the course! It was a Donald Ross design, and for my money, he beats the pants off of Pete Dye's designs. Remember, Pete Dye is the guy who designed TPC at Sawgrass, where I had a nightmare golf experience paying a significant sum of money to get beat to death by a golf course. This place was one-third the cost and 100 times the pleasure for its pure beauty and magnificent design. Donald Ross has done over a hundred golf courses in America and is considered one of the best designers ever. He has many of his courses in the top 100 in this country. Look him up on Google, and they will list his creations. Anyway, this is one of the best I have seen of his; it might be his masterpiece.

Mark Ritchie and Pat Becker were two guys from Bull Valley Golf Course in Woodstock, Illinois. It is where they filmed *Groundhog Day*, my favorite movie. I thought that the movie was filmed in Punxsutawney, PA. But apparently, it was filmed in Woodstock and made to appear it was in Punxsutawney. They are members at Bull Valley, and their pro arranged for them to play at Augusta Country Club. Mark Ritchie was nice; he bought me a shirt with the Augusta Country Club logo and lunch. What a good guy, but more importantly, what a lovely thing to do for someone. Including a stranger in their golf day was lucky, and I greatly appreciated it. I must follow his example and do a good thing like that for someone else and pay it forward. Acts of kindness like that are genuinely heartwarming things. I learned a lot from his act. He was just a lovely person. Pat was also very nice but a bit more reserved than Mark.

I played a good round of golf from the Blue Tees and shot an 84 from 6600 yards. In case some of you don't know what I am talking about, each golf course has different levels of difficulty based on the distance one plays from. If you play from the back, they are the Championship tees, and a club championship would be played from there, or if the course is big time, then the pros play from the longest tees. The next set of tees is the next difficulty level with one or two more levels. For the women, there is usually just one set of tees. In the case of this country club, there were also the white tees (6215 yards), then the green tees (5484 yards). The Red Tees are the ladies' tees; they were 5124 yards at this course. The golf course is a links-style golf course, meaning that the holes are linked together, and you play nine holes out and then nine holes back, like St. Andrews Golf Course in Scotland. People don't realize the influence of the Scots architects like Donald Ross in the South. Their work on golf courses is well known. It is a long history in America, and I will not bore you with it.

I had planned to play just three courses on this trip, and this one was just a bonus. I am so lucky. Even though we walked the eighteen holes, I had a blast playing today. If you don't know Augusta, Georgia, it is in the hills, and the golf courses are very hilly. I cannot believe how many times we walked uphill to the greens. The course was a typical Donald Ross design. This year, the US Open is being played at Pinehurst #2 in Pinehurst, North Carolina, and it is a Donald Ross design. I have played it twice, and it is beautiful, but I think Augusta Country Club is better and prettier. Playing here was just icing on the cake of my travels.

PART 3:

AUGUSTA, GEORGIA TO HELLERTOWN, PENNSYLVANIA

MAY 25, 2014

Driving from Augusta to Nashville was quite a trip because it was a Friday holiday, and I knew the Atlanta traffic would delay me. It did. I stopped just outside Atlanta to get some gas; the station had a car wash attached. It was a hand wash done by three young guys for 12 dollars. My car was pelted with bugs in Florida, so I had to get them off. One of the guys worked diligently on the front of the car for a long time, and he noticed I was from California. So once he finished everything, I rolled down the window because he had questions. He and his buddies gathered around and looked at me like I was from Mars because I was from California.

"You drive all that way?" "How much is gas in California?" "Is the price of living very expensive in California?" I hear they pay 10.75 an hour to work at McDonalds and only pay 7.75 here." They were fun and funny as they gossiped about what they had heard about the famous California, and I was their answer to the questions. One of them had heard that gas was 5 dollars a gallon, and I said it could get close to that in some places in California. Anyway, the guy continued to work on my car and did the wheels and all the critical details of the car. I gave him 20 bucks because he worked hard to make it look good. I don't say that to be a troll but to indicate that I appreciate someone willing to work. I like people who have good work ethics. It is how I see the difference between one person and another. I don't care for lazy, non-producing people looking for a handout for doing nothing.

Driving as far as I have has taught me something about the behavior of the highway patrol in all states. The chief characteristic is that they do not wait at the top of the hill to measure how fast you are going, but they wait at the bottom. They nail you if you speed down a hill, so I learned to take my foot off the accelerator as I went downhill and always stay in the right lane so they know I am not looking to speed. I cannot tell you how many people I have seen pulled over during my trip, but it was tons. Some people defy the odds and speed up to eighty plus miles per hour on these highways. I would instead take longer and arrive later than get a speeding ticket. But watch out, they are waiting at the bottom of the hill most of the time. And they hide, too. They are in the trees, lurking in the grass, and behind barriers, so they are there to catch you. Drive safely and close to the speed limit. It is posted at 70 in most places, and in some places, it is 75. It varies.

I saw another sign near Atlanta that read "Wing and Fish." It was a restaurant looking to lure people in with their sign. It would have been more inviting had it said "Wings and Fish." At least one knows that you will get more than one wing. I had to stop for dinner because it was getting late, and I turned off to a highway exit I had never seen before! It had every conceivable fast-food restaurant in the country! McDonald's, Taco Bell, Burger King, Hardees (Carl's version back east), Chick-fil-A, and several others!! It is incredible; as I have said, we are a fast-food country. I ate at a place called Shoney's, and it was a buffet-style Southern place that had some excellent fish and a great salad for only 10.95. I got in and out in less than 25 minutes. I was in a hurry.

If you want to throw trash out the window in Georgia, it will cost you a one thousand dollar fine, so be careful when you open a window as you don't want a piece of paper flying out of the car. They are earnest about this! I found the roadsides to be clean and pretty. Georgia is quite beautiful, but Tennessee is even better with the green mountains and the beautiful vistas.

It is Memorial Day weekend and a time to recognize the service of our veterans. I listened to a discussion with the author of a book on the Vietnam War and the Battle of Khe Sanh and remembered the different treatment that soldiers got returning from that war than they are today. Today, the common comment is "Thanks for your service," whereas the anger and protest against the Vietnam War were so pronounced that returning soldiers were disregarded and even spat upon. It was not a choice for those who were drafted into that war, and I am reminded of my own "good luck" when I got to the end of the line after my physical for being drafted, and a doctor looked at me and said, "You are a 4-F young man." "Why?" I inquired. You have vitiligo (a skin pigmentation), giving you a 4-F status, meaning I was ineligible to serve. In a sense, I had dodged a bullet with my pun fully intended. I got back home and signed up for graduate school.

I was on my way to becoming a teacher. It was a good choice of a career and one I will never regret. I taught students about the Vietnam War and the protests at the time. They wanted to know about it. Today, if you know a Vietnam Veteran, tell him, "Thanks for the service." Thanks, Robert Sorensen, Tom Luginbill, Don Lyons, and all I forget. It was a war that many fine young men gave their lives for. When I visit the Vietnam War Memorial in Washington, DC, I will relate more about it.

MAY 26, 2014

I rolled into Nashville, Tennessee, late Friday night but got up by 8 o'clock to explore Nashville. I went to the downtown area and found parking was costly at fifteen dollars for two hours, so I set the meter for three hours and walked around the area and saw many of the essential music buildings for the music industry as well as where there are many great performances of music by the country singers of the day.

Walking down Broadway Street, I saw many people preparing to become performers at bigger venues. There is a lot of talent in the city, and it is so hard to make oneself known in a world where those who are just average are nothing. I found many young people standing on the streets strumming the guitar, singing to themselves, and looking for a handout. At eleven A.M., many young people drank and listened to aspiring country music singers in the bars. They've had to have been to fifty or so of these places, and one has to wonder how they came to make any money with all that competition. There were lots of people starting to show up, but I found that the city is very punitive with the parking, and even the public parking lots are pretty much the same cost. So how does one stay in that area for any time and not pay a fortune for parking? And they warn you that the parking is strictly enforced, one can end up with a ticket on top of the parking charges. I watched it closely and never got enough time to explore the area thoroughly. I had a function to go to anyway. Nashville is where all the prospective new singers go to try and make it big.

My sister-in-law, Debby Sinay, is married to my brother Gary. She has a son, Tommy, who is married to Marsha Zurawicki. They live just West of Nashville, so I was invited to the graduation party of Marsha's sister, Ola, who is fifteen years younger than Marsha. Marsha and Ola have another sister, Molly, who is about two years older than Marsha. Molly and her husband, Andrew, have four wonderful kids, and Marsha and Tommy have two little adorable girls, Scarlet and Madeline.

Walter Zurawicki is the father, and his wife's name is Christina, and they are a remarkable American success story. They came to America from Poland in 1983 with just four hundred dollars in their pocket and no ability to speak English. Through hard work and dedication to family, Walter eventually built up a business and another business to accomplish the American Dream of owning one's own home.

I found a wonderful family inviting me like a group member into the house. When I entered the door, Walter Zurawicki gave me a big bear hug and told me I was welcome to stay as long as I wanted. I then had the best time learning about the different stories of each of the three girls in the family. Despite being immigrants, Molly and Marsha earned degrees from college and were honors students in high school. Ola had just graduated from high school and was the Salutatorian. She was planning to go to Evanston College in Illinois. This party celebrated her graduation, a big deal for the Zurawicki family. I loved to see that they valued education, which many 3rd, 4th, and 5th-generation Americans can learn from this first generation of Americans---education is essential.

I was about to leave around 7:30 when one of the sisters, Marsha, told me that her dad would be offended if I left that early. I didn't want to overstay my welcome. As the night wore on, I learned that Walter was involved with the Solidarity Movement in Poland during the Lech Walesa era. He was nearly his right-hand man. I saw some pictures of him and Lech in the front room. Walter became, for me, a very fascinating man. As the night wore on, Walter told many stories, and I laughed until I cried; he was so funny. Walter is a big, burly man with a booming voice who held nothing back when he spoke his mind. He was living his dream, and now his third daughter is going to college to get her education and make a life for herself in America.

It was a heartwarming story, and by the end of the night, after several drinks of various ethnic derivations, I was hugging the whole family goodbye and getting a ride back to my hotel from Tommy Smith, who was smart enough to pick me up there and know I would need a ride by the end of the night. What a party, a family, and a day with the Zurawicki family in Kingston Springs, TN. They were the epitome of The American Dream. It is still alive.

MAY 27, 2014

I drove from Nashville, Tennessee, to Canton, Ohio, where I was born, to see some of the many cousins I still have in this Football Hall of Fame town. Before I got to Canton, just South of the city was a little village called Zoar, where my cousins lived when I was a little tyke. They were my cousins on the mother's side from her sister Julie Labak Orzeck, married to Joe Orzeck. My mother's maiden name was Labak.

Thomas Wolfe, the American author, said in his famous novel *You Can't Go Home Again:*

> "You can't go back home to your family, back home to your childhood, back home to romantic love, back home to a young man's dreams of glory and of fame, back home to exile, to escape to Europe and some foreign land, back home to lyricism, to singing just for singing's sake, back home to aestheticism, to one's youthful idea of 'the artist' and the all-sufficiency of 'art' and 'beauty' and 'love,' back home to the ivory tower, back home to places in the country, to the cottage in Bermuda, away from all the strife and conflict of the world, back home to the father you have lost and have been looking for, back home to someone who can help you, save you, ease

the burden for you, back home to the old forms and systems of things which once seemed everlasting but which are changing all the time--back home to the escapes of Time and Memory."

Wolfe said we can't go back in time to relive warm, pleasant memories of those times, even by going to the actual physical location we called home in our youth. I went into that tavern in Zoar, Ohio, and got such a nostalgic feeling and remembered the days we spent there visiting the cousins and laughing and playing and living in such an innocent time. We did not read about young people taking a gun, driving up and down the street in Isla Vista, near UC Santa Barbara, and slaughtering several innocent people. We lived in a much more innocent time then, and it was a time I just as soon have back. But Thomas Wolfe is right. I can't get back what I want and what I had then. I am only trying to tell my cousins a little knowledge about our heritage that I discovered through Ancestry. com. I am not trying to go back to my past so much as I am trying to discover what it was and share it with those who may want to know.

After my research from ancestry.com was completed, I learned that my ethnicity is one hundred percent Slovakian for the first time in my life. I only knew this once I had the Ancestry people find out the exact birthplaces of my four grandparents, and it turns out they were all born in Slovakia. I am a second-generation full Slovakian, a real rarity. My dad was born in Canonsburg, Pennsylvania, and is a first-generation Slovakian in America. My grandfather and grandmother on my dad's side came to America in 1909 with three children and a place to work in the steel mills of Pennsylvania. One of the three children, my Uncle Stephen, died of complications sixteen days after he arrived in America. They took him off the boat at Hoffman Island before my grandmother went to Ellis Island with the other two children. I am eternally grateful for my grandfather's courage to bring his family to America. For the ten children that he and his wife would have, it meant a better life for them in America, and many of the children of those ten children (there are 39 first cousins on dad's side) have managed a college education and a better life for themselves. Now, the cousins are spread over the country, and I have been trying to connect with them as I take my "bucket list" ancestry journey across the country.

So even though Thomas Wolfe said, "You can't go home again," I am trying to do so. I met a cousin last night, James Sinay, and told him that my grandson has the same name. He was thrilled—another James Sinay. So I spent the evening with Jim and had a wonderful time. We laughed about the time my brother and I went to Las Vegas and had a great time with Jim at his place. He had a picture of the event. Jim was a dealer of various games at casinos in Las Vegas and is about to publish a book called "Confessions of a Las Vegas Casino Dealer." He had a lot of exciting stories about Las Vegas when the Mob was running the city. He slept at night with a gun under his pillow. Now, the corporations all own the town, and after a forty-year career there, he returned to Canton, Ohio, to live out his remaining days.

I am looking forward to reading the book and seeing a potential movie made about some of the stories he has told in the book. I learned Jim was an excellent singer and was amazed at listening to him do Karaoke at a local hangout. He sounded so much like my dad's singing.

So, I guess I can't expect things to be as they were when I was younger. I spent just twelve years here in Canton, Ohio, and I am back to see the changes and the home where my life started.

MAY 28, 2014

Today, I went back home. I met my cousin, Jerry Sinay, who took me to my childhood home. I went home to 1655 Stark Avenue in Southwest Canton, where I spent the first twelve years of my life.

The reason why anyone "can't go home again," as Thomas Wolfe was saying, is simply that things change, and they will never be the same again. It is what Holden Caulfield struggled with in his life: change. Holden was the main character in the J.D. Salinger novel *The Catcher in the Rye.* Holden hated change and knew they would never be the same again once things changed. That is why he wanted to be "the catcher in the rye" to catch the kids from falling off the cliff as they ran through the Rye fields. Holden hated change. When he saw his sister Phoebe going round and round on the carousel at the amusement park, he started bawling his eyes out because he knew nothing would change as long as she was going round and round.

But life is constantly changing, isn't it? Things don't stay the same. Or, as Robert Frost put it, "Nothing Gold Can Stay." His poem says the same thing. Things changed, and that is a fact of life. We may not change, but circumstances change, and we find ourselves readjusting. We find ourselves on a different track than what we were on before. If Eden did not stay the same, innocence would be lost again. As a day passes into night, nothing is the same as when the day started. Here is Frost's poem:

"Nothing Gold Can Stay"

Nature's first green is gold,
Her hardest hue to hold.
Her early leaf's a flower;
But only so an hour.
The leaf subsides to leaf.
So Eden sank to grief,
So dawn goes down to day.
Nothing gold can stay.

As we toured the neighborhood, the Catholic school Sacred Heart, where I attended as a child, was gone. It was beautiful to have my older cousin take me to this area and teach me what I was looking at. The school was gone, but the church was still there that I used to walk to in the snow as a kid and serve mass. It was a Catholic church in my day and now a Christian Fellowship church. I was amazed to see the house where the priest resided at Sacred Heart was still standing. The house where the nuns resided was also there.

We drove up and down the streets where I hung out as a kid, and I found a lot of poverty and a very chaotic neighborhood with some houses still the same as they were fifty years ago. I was amazed at how small and shabby this area was. It is truly a poverty area. Near this area was the famous Timken Roller Bearing Company, which had been there when I was a child. I was amazed at the ball-bearing plant and how it has survived all these years.

1655 STARK AVENUE: MY CHILDHOOD HOME

At one time, the neighborhood was riddled with mom-and-pop grocery stores and bars. I could not believe how many of these little grocery stores there were, and even though my grandfather had run the grocery store that was our house, he had survived the 20s, 30s, and 40s before handing it over to his daughter, my mother. My mother and father ran the grocery store for some years, but I did not learn how long it was. The store was defunct when I was seven or eight years old.

Jerry then took me downtown in Canton to see what it looked like. I thought that it was the biggest city in the world when I was small and just a ten-year-old. It was not that big, but it was amazing to see. I had never really seen Timken High School, where my brother and sister graduated from, and I had never seen McKinley High School, where my mother had graduated from in 1935. I saw both and several vital parts of the town, especially the movie theater where we used to see movies as kids, a mere twenty-five cents for two movies. Today, I can spend twenty-five dollars for one IMAX movie for two people! How times have changed and how difficult it is to go home again.

I had lunch with Jerry at Baker's Cafe down the street from where I lived, and we had one great conversation after another. It is so lovely to be able to learn about the lives of other cousins. Jerry was a great conversationalist and a great listener. I enjoyed his company, and we had such a good time; we returned to his house and talked until nearly nine p.m. He has a beautiful house in Louisville, north of Canton. He had seven kids; it was so lovely to see pictures of them. We sat out on the front porch of his house and had many topics slip through the fingers of our minds. I found that, like other cousins, he had a good sense of humor. He loved hearing a good joke or making a funny comment and laughed that familiar Sinay laugh. He loved learning about the family's history, everything I had to say about grandma and grandpa, and what I had learned about their lives.

JERRY SINAY'S HOME IN LOUISVILLE, OHIO

It was a great time, but time passed, and things changed, and I had to move on to the other cousins and try to go home again. I saw a picture of Tiger Woods on the wall in our booth, saying he loved coming to Baker's Restaurant. He frequented the place when he played at the South Course at Firestone Country Club. It was first known as the WGC NEC Invitational, and Woods won it in year one and then went on to win it seven more times.

MAY 29, 2014

I continued to try to go home again by visiting some places that were important to me. As I set out to see some of the sights of Canton, I found myself thinking of other things that occurred during my time here in my youth. So I had to go there and see where I first fell in love and the place that also meant so much pain. When I went to elementary school at Sacred Heart Catholic School in Southwest Canton, it was announced that the school was unsafe and that we would have to take a bus to another school the following year. We were bused to St. Anthony's school on the city's Southeast side for our sixth-grade year. We were placed in a classroom with the fifth graders in the same room. There were probably thirty-five students for the two grades. I got there and noticed an additional building I was not sure was there when I attended.

I spoke with a lady working outside, and she thought it would be acceptable to go inside. It was the school I attended for one miserable year. It was miserable because the boys who had already been at the school felt that the new Sacred Heart boys were invading their space. When some girls were interested in us, it set the other boys off. They were Tommy Martin, Gus Guzzo, and Ronnie Boni. We got beat up by these guys daily, and it was done when the nuns were not looking. It ended when my mother finally called the school and let them have it. The nuns were mad at us because the priests chewed them out for not protecting the Sacred Heart boys. This ended, and we were relieved.

Before we left school on our last day, one of the boys fought at the bus stop with my brother, Tom. That fat pig Gus Guzzo pushed Tom around like he was nothing. We were small kids. We were more relieved when we learned that we were moving to California. It is horrible to be bullied at school, and as a teacher for many years, I was susceptible to anyone bullying another kid. I warned my students about such behavior at the beginning of my class; it never happened in my classroom in thirty-seven years.

ST. ANTHONY'S SCHOOL IN CANTON, OHIO

Many years later, I contacted one of them through Facebook. When I had the chance, I discussed what he and his two friends did to us at that school. I told the guy I would probably knock his head off if I encountered him. He tried to tell me what a good Christian he was now that he was an adult. Although he was sorry for his horrible treatment of us, he still did not understand how damaging bullying is to a young person. I told him and his two buddies they should go to hell for their brutal treatment of us.

While at St. Anthony's, I had a "girlfriend" named Barbara Dolf. She was this cute blond in the next row, and I always passed her notes. I remember once when we were down in the basement where there was the cafeteria, we ditched in a back area and hugged. I was in love. That is about as serious as it got. But I would go to sleep at night and think of her. We never said goodbye when I left school because it was a bitter departure for us. I was sorry about that.

The final thing I do remember was that this school seemed like a very long way from home, and it was. It was over two and a half miles as I measured the distance by driving from St. Anthony's to my home on Stark Avenue. Getting home after school was sometimes challenging because it was a walk through some undesirable neighborhoods. When I had to do it, it was pretty scary. I cannot believe my parents made me walk home from time to time in that circumstance. It was too far for an 11-year-old kid.

I then spent time at the Canton Hall of Fame for Football and learned about why the Football Hall of Fame was situated in Canton. It was because the first professional teams included the Canton Bulldogs. They won the first two football championships. Visiting the Hall of Fame was quite exciting and quite enjoyable. It is filled with stuff that covers the whole history of football. It was quite an experience to see the history of football. It is one of the country's best Sports Hall of Fame venues.

HALL OF FAME FOR FOOTBALL IN CANTON, OHIO

I also wanted to see the McKinley Memorial and the Presidential Library and Museum. William McKinley had the misfortune of being one of the presidents who was assassinated, but almost nobody knows who assassinated him and why. This is his story:

Leon Frank Czolgosz believed there was a great injustice in American society, an inequality that allowed the wealthy to enrich themselves by exploiting the poor. He concluded that the reason for this was the structure of government itself. Then he learned of a European crime, which changed his life: On July 29, 1900, King Umberto I of Italy had been shot dead by anarchist Gaetano Bresci. Bresci told the press that he had decided to take matters into his own hands for the sake of the common man. This is what motivated Leon Cxolgosz to take action.

The assassination shocked and galvanized the American anarchist movement, and Czolgosz is thought to have consciously imitated Bresci. New York police officer Joseph Petrosino believed that the same group had previously targeted President McKinley, but his warnings were useless because McKinley ignored them. Perhaps the most disturbing part of McKinley's assassination was that he had poor doctor care.

McKinley was a native of Canton, and his memorial is the largest in the country for a president. McKinley was a good, honest man, but he reigned during the Gilded Age, and there are a lot of similarities between that era and our own. It is one of the reasons I wanted to see his story, but it was also because the high school my mother attended was named after him. More importantly, are we always in the Gilded Age, where barons and wealthy people subdue the middle and lower classes to do their bidding? George Carlin, A modern day humorist, said that is precisely what is happening.

MCKINLEY MEMORIAL IN CANTON, OHIO

The museum also had a history of Canton, Ohio, and it was somewhat interesting. Timken Roller Bearing Company has been here for six decades and has survived because all cars need these bearings. That is why the other high school my brother and sister attended was named after the original man who started the Timken Roller Bearing Company. Today, the same family runs the company.

My final destination today was to visit the gravesite of my grandparents, Andrew and Rosalie Sinay. I found them residing at Calvary Cemetery in Massillon, Ohio, about 20 minutes from where I lived when I was young. I found their grave, stood over it for some time, and reflected on their sacrifices to come to America and their journey when they came. After having ten children and trying to bring them up during the Depression, I am sure they wondered if coming to America was a better place than what they had left in Slovakia. I am sure they thought life would be better. However, the American Dream was not there for many years. Most children were born in the 1910s and grew up in the 20s and 30s. These were tough times in America. Now they rest in the beautiful cemetery with the wind blowing briskly through the trees, and a calm and a peace came over me, knowing that I had come all the way home, looking down at the grave and seeing the name Sinay scrolled across the stone.

MAY 30, 2014

Today was another cousin day, so I traveled to Northeast Canton to see my cousin, whom I had not seen in 54 years. She was an absolute doll. No wonder. Her name is Dolly Sinay Hussar, and she was the daughter of my Uncle John and Aunt Virginia. They had four children, and I have already discussed her brother, Jerry Sinay. Dolly and I went to lunch, talked, and never stopped for five hours. We covered it all and the lives of those important to us. We delved into the past, and I asked questions that even she could not answer, but they are questions I may never be able to get answers to.

I wanted to know what my grandfather did when he came to America. I wanted to fill in that time gap before I knew what he did for a living. Dolly did not know what Grandpa Sinay did when he first came to America, and that was that. I did not expect her to know this, but since she was one of the older cousins, I was hoping she did. Anyway, I learned an interesting thing about the Sinay family. As the reader knows, there were ten children on my father's side, and each of them got married, and for a while, they were all in the same vicinity of Canton, Ohio. During that time, pictures of the entire family could be taken, and one was taken on the 40th anniversary of Grandma and Grandpa in 1944. I learned it was taken at the Slovak Club in Southwest Canton, where we lived, and Grandma and Grandpa lived. It was on the stage at the Slovak Club that it was taken.

What the picture symbolizes is the unity of the family and how families were together in those days. Everyone lived in the same vicinity and could be with their cousins and have fun together. This was the time when America had unity in families. But before long, changes started to take place. First, my Uncle Bill Sinay and Aunt Guernile took their family to California around 1958. Then, my dad got an excellent job in Compton, California, in 1960, so we moved there. The family started to spread out. Eventually, others would move away from Canton. Yet, some stayed. When Grandma and Grandpa died, the families started to be more alone. The extended family was forgotten. We had some reunions as time passed, and they were efforts to bind the family together, if only for a little while again. Then came all the first cousins who started to go to college and would end up working where they went to college, and there was more dissemination of the family. The readers get the picture. Things change. It is hard to go home again. One wonders if the breaking out and the breaking up of the family is the foundation of our troubles these days. It is curious to think about what it would be like if people could stay in their communities, grow up, and find a job. That is still done today, but it is becoming less and less so. And I think of the demise of everything.

I discovered that there are twins in each of the first three generations of the Sinay family. I have twin uncles, and I am one of the twin cousins. Some of the first cousins had twins, including twin second cousins. Twins are in the family, and they continue to show up occasionally. So it was interesting to learn that the twin gene can pop up anywhere, and it was fun to learn that the twin thing was still running around in the family.

Like any big family, there are going to be problems, and there are going to be conflicts. There were conflicts between some of the people who came into the family. My dad said there were in-laws and outlaws in families. And he did not mean that those who married into the family were necessarily outlaws. Outlaws could come from within the family itself. I learned this was the case in my father's generation and among his nine brothers and sisters. And I know it has been a problem in the first cousin generation where members or new family members became outcasts. There are numerous reasons for this, and it would be silly to surmise that it is only one reason, but it happens in every generation. If the next generation were still in touch with one another, there would be problems with different people in that group. I know that it is just human nature and that some are destined to be outlaws in the family, whether initially in the family or not.

So I drove home from my cousin Dolly's house feeling good just having the opportunity to know one more of my first cousins for a little while and to disseminate some more knowledge and information about the origin of the Sinay name. I learned that many of the cousins need to be made aware of the origin of the name, and it may take a while to learn that. I thought of the play *Our Town* by Thornton Wilder when I was at the cemetery the other day. In that play, the author has a young lady die, and then the young lady has the opportunity to come back to life and experience the family for one day. She sees her mother and father going through their daily routine, and she tries to tell them to look at me for a while and see me. But they cannot crack out of their mold, and they cannot crack out of their routine in life. Stop and listen to what I am saying, and learn that life is short, life is precious, and life should be lived at every moment one can. It is a family that one has to enjoy and stay together with. After a while, we run out of these moments and become a part of Calvary Cemetery, looking at those still alive but asleep in life. Wake up tomorrow, enjoy every moment, live, and love life. It is the only one you have here on earth.

MAY 31, 2014

Today was special because my cousins went out of their way to be there for me to see them. There was the Seibert family, whose mother, Dorthy Sinay Seibert, was the last child on my father's side; in short, she was child number ten. Today, I met Greg, Dan, and Mark Seibert, three of the sons. Also, I first met Karen, Greg's wife, and Melissa, Mark's wife. We spent much time talking about the family and where each cousin resides. More importantly, we just spent a lot of time laughing at different situations. It is just amazing that the laughter trait permeates the family. What I learned by meeting these three cousins is that we all have things that show up in our bodies that have been in there from the genetic makeup of our parents. And it is true. We get what our parents and our grandparents had. And it can come to one kid in the family more than it can come to another family member. There is no justice to genetics. I am talking about the trait of laughter, and I am talking about the problems with disease and other disorders passed on through the generations. There is only hope that one can prevent or work around the problem.

COUSINS GREG, MARK, DAN AND RANDY SEIBERT

I had a great time meeting Karen Seibert, Greg's wife, because she is the one that inspired me to do a lot of work on our family history. I wanted to learn more about my grandfather's work when he came to America, and I found on the 1920 Census that he listed himself as employed at an "Iron Mill." So, he did the same work in Pennsylvania as in Ohio, so when he took the family to Ohio, he was hired by Republic Steel in Canton. It was common for people to work for steel companies in those days since we had some of the best steel companies in the world. I currently live part-time in Pennsylvania near one of the most famous steel mills in the country, Bethlehem Steel. It no longer functions in any capacity, so making steel is still a part of the American scene, except it has seen better days. The zenith of making steel has long passed for America. It is one of those things that have changed.

Meeting my cousins from Aunt Dorothy Sinay and Uncle Lee Seibert was gratifying. I was able to be with Aunt Dorothy more because Uncle Lee died at the early age of fifty-five. They were one of the sets of cousins to lose a parent early. And I look at the ten sets of aunts and uncles on my father's side, and I see that one passed at the early age of fifty and her husband is still alive at ninety-seven, then it shows how random the "ringing of the bell" can be. (or as John Donne said, "Never send to know for whom the bell tolls, it tolls for thee.") I am so grateful for having two parents who lived well into their 80s because I got to share a lot of time with them and say what I wanted to say to them. I never regretted their passing because I did not lose either unexpectedly. Not everyone can say that; I feel for those with different and more troubling situations. I know seeing those who lost their parents too early is painful.

I spent three or more hours with the Seiberts, but that was a sliver of time. I learned much from them about Canton, and I was not there at those times. I also committed Karen to continue to improve the family tree on ancestry.com. The next phase is to put in videos and pictures that future generations can see. I am looking forward to working on that.

I then went to Wadsworth, Ohio, about thirty minutes away, where I met three cousins on my mother's side and learned much about that side of the family. My first cousin, Father Joe Labak, is the son of Joe and Helen Labak, my mother's youngest brother. My mother's maiden name was Labak. Labak is also a Slovakian name.

Father Joe had three siblings: Helen, Vicki, and Michael. Helen's husband was Martin "Marty" James Zemanek, a good Slovak name and a lovely man. Vicky's husband was August "Al" John Kipovsky, another great Slovak name and a very good man.

As the reader may recall, I met their brother, Michael Labak, in Charlestown, South Carolina. It was beautiful to see this, and I learned how involved they were in the Sokols, a fraternity of Slovaks, but a fraternity opening up to other ethnicities. It was interesting. The cousins were adorable, and so were the husbands. Some of their children have stayed close to where they live while others have moved away, so my argument that the family is spreading out more and more holds to some degree. It was nice to be with three of the four children of my mother's youngest brother. We ate at a restaurant run by Serbians, and they made chicken like I had never eaten chicken before. It was fried ala Southern style, but better. The whole group raved about it, and everyone ordered the chicken. They gave three sides with the chicken and enough to feed two people.

During the dinner, I learned that my grandmother on my mother's side was illegitimate, like my grandfather on my father's side. What? It was a shocker, but my cousin Father Joe had been to Slovakia several times to research the Labak side of the family. Anyway, my genealogist will not believe it when she gets the documents for birth and baptism. I am still getting the data from the genealogist, and she has not said that yet, but eventually, she will. I await her to discover this problem and realize my grandmother's name is Sabel, not Zahumensky. That is what her sister's name was. It was known that her sister was born legitimately with Frank Zuhmensky and her mother. Anyway, learning the truth about my grandparent's origins has been an exciting ride. I have learned that truth is not as obvious as one thinks, and as one writer put it, "Truth is a hard deer to hunt."

I had a wonderful time, although a brief time, with my cousins in Wadsworth, Ohio. This was near the town of Barberton, where they grew up as kids. We did not see them as often as the other cousins, and I am not sure why that was. It was just that way, but I found them genuine and beautiful and missed having enough time with them. Father Joe then drove me back to his parish, and we sat and chatted for a while. What I came to learn about the family on my mother's side was good news. At least all of my grandparents were born in the same country. Father Joe was a kind and welcoming host, and he must have thanked me several times for buying everyone's dinner at the restaurant we were together at. It was nothing. I wanted to share what I had at that moment with my long-ago missing cousins. I did not have enough time with them, but they were wonderful people. Then I told Father Joe I had to take pictures of his parish and make him famous. He graciously accepted.

FATHER JOE LABAK IN WADSWORTH, OHIO

So I had finished with the cousins in Canton, Ohio, and I had seen ten of them and felt lucky to be able to do that. I had gone home to see if I could find out more about myself, my ethnicity, and my cousins. I had accomplished all three. And even though Thomas Wolfe says, "You can't go home again," I suppose one can try, and through the effort, one discovers more of who one is and becomes just a little more at peace with life.

JUNE 1, 2014

Today, as far as I know, I left Canton, Ohio, for the last time in my life, but it has been a wonderful experience. I decided to go to Canonsburg, Pennsylvania, where it all started. That is where my paternal grandfather and grandmother came to when they came from Slovakia. I learned in Canton that my grandfather worked in an "Iron Mill" in Canonsburg, but I had an address where they lived when they were there. So I put the address in the GPS, and off I went to see the original residence in America of the Sinay family.

When I arrived at the location of the address I had, I found that the house was no longer there, but many of the houses from the same era were still there, so I took pictures of them while I drove around and looked at the ambiance of Canonsburg. It was a dilapidated city, and it had seen a better day. It was once a thriving community with people who worked in the steel industry, but it fell apart when that industry left town. It is like so many cities in this country that have had the employment of the town move either to another state or another country. What is left behind is a shell of a town, a skeleton with not much meat on it anymore. It is troubling to see that here in America, and I suppose most people don't care or think about it unless it affects them. When one sees the deterioration of the towns, one begins to wonder if our country is on the right or wrong path. Have corporations sold out America by moving all our manufacturing jobs overseas? Are all these jobs elsewhere that are not benefiting America and Americans? Where are the new jobs to come from? I have an economist friend, Peter Navarro, a professor of economics at UCI or the University of California at Irvine, and he claims that we need to reinstitute the manufacturing jobs in this country for us to be whole again. We have shipped our middle-class working jobs overseas so corporations can earn a more significant profit. When I saw Cannonsburg, I saw what that does to an American community–it destroys it.

TYPICAL HOME IN CANONSBURG, PA

I spent an hour touring the city and saw the Catholic Church, where my grandparents and the kids went for Sunday mass. I saw the neighborhoods, the parks, the banks, and other churches, and I could not help but think that it must have been a good yet still challenging time in their lives. It was different from the place where rich people lived. However, I am eternally grateful for the risk my grandfather took when he brought his three children and his wife over from Slovakia. I realized what a strange place this must have been for those who did not speak English yet could connect with those who came over with them. Ethnic groups lived in the same neighborhoods, and sometimes, there was a mixture, but many stuck together for comfort and recognition.

It was indicated in the shipping record that my grandfather came to be with a cousin of his named Johann Durkac. I have yet to make a connection between him and my grandfather, but I did have a genealogist work on the connection in Slovakia. He claims that there is no connection, but my genealogist here in Salt Lake City, Utah, thinks there is, but it always takes more money to find the answer to that question. I am unsure if I can commit more money to that project, given that I am doing another project verifying the grandparents on my mother's side. I suppose I will cross that bridge when I get to it. Carole Chi, one of my favorite supporters, wants to see if I can officially establish that connection to call her cousin. She is a descendent of the Durkac family and calls me "cuz." She is in Michigan and wants me to drop by on the way back home on my trip back West. I told her I would try.

JUNE 2, 2014

The following day, I drove across Pennsylvania to Hellertown, a small town in the eastern part of the state. Hellertown is where my sweetheart, Nancy DeVogel, lives. It is an old, but tiny town in America. Nancy and I were a couple in high school and our first year and a half of college before we split apart. She ended up on the East Coast, and I stayed in California. We lost contact in June of 1968 and discovered one another in the fall of 2003. After a lengthy email relationship, I decided to get divorced and spend more time with her. My relationship at home had failed after twenty-five years together with my ex-wife. I left my home in Irvine in the summer of 2004, and it has now been ten years since I have been going back and forth from California to Pennsylvania.

It took me five hours to drive across the state to Hellertown, and it was just in time to pick up Nancy and continue the trip around the country. Because she was still working, she could not make the whole trip with me, so our trip together back east was planned before I got there. Our next segment of the trip will be to see all those literary authors I taught in high school and college. I wanted to see more of where they lived and how they lived. I got there in the afternoon, and Nancy and I talked until we retired for the evening. I told her all about my adventures.

PART 4

HELLERTOWN, PENNSYLVANIA TO ELMIRA, NEW YORK

JUNE 5TH, 2014

Nancy and I embarked on our literary journey early in the morning to get to Perkasie, Pennsylvania, and visit the home of Pearl S. Buck. The only connection to Ms. Buck was reading her novel, *The Good Earth* when I was a freshman in high school. Reading the book took place long ago, but I remember that it drove me to want to read more. In the early 1960s, when I entered high school, it was assumed that one could read at grade level. English teachers at that time knew nothing about reading and reading levels. Aside from reading *The Good Earth*, we read *The Red Pony* by John Steinbeck, *The Heart of Darkness* and the *Secret Sharer* by Joseph Conrad, and Sir Walter Scott's *Ivanhoe*. We also read George Orwell's *Animal Farm*, William Shakespeare's *Romeo and Juliet*, *The Iliad*, and *The Odyssey*. One would have thought we were prepping for Harvard. Although we did have students who went to Yale, Harvard, and Stanford from our graduating class, these books were for "average" classes. There are few schools in the country where such a curriculum exists. For many different reasons, students today would not be able to handle that level of reading or have any willingness to do so. I taught for thirty-seven years at the high school level and could not get my honors students to handle that curriculum. The National Assessment of Educational Progress, a long-term study of academic progress in American education, has indicated that "The aggregate of all of the resources, initiatives, policies, and programs the United States has implemented for K-12 school reform has not had a corresponding impact on improving reading proficiency. The impact has been virtually nonexistent over the past 40-plus years."

Pearl Buck's home in Perkasie, Pennsylvania, was just gorgeous. The extensive libraries that she had were so impressive. Her parents took her to China when she was just three months old, and she spent nearly forty years in China, living in Zhenjiang with her parents and Nanjing with her first husband. She then spent forty years in Perkasie at Green Hills Farms estate before retiring in Danby, Vermont, where she died on March 6, 1973. She was born in Hillsboro, West Virginia, on June 26, 1892.

PEARL BUCK HOME IN PERKASIE, PENNSYLVANNIA

Although she won the Nobel Prize for literature and was the first American woman to do so, most of her work is unrecognized except *The Good Earth*. Visiting her estate was more the pleasure of seeing her beautiful house and the spacious grounds where the house is located. It is truly magnificent and worth the effort to see. We went through the tour of the house and the presentations and learned what a great humanitarian she was. I learned that her name, Pearl, came from the novel *The Scarlet Letter* by Nathaniel Hawthorne, another writer we will manage to see on this trip.

From the very first time we see Pearl, she symbolizes adultery. The name "Pearl" comes from Hester as a reminder of her sin: "But she named the infant 'Pearl' as being of great price,--purchased with all she had,--her mother's only treasure!" (Hawthorne 168). Perhaps Pearl Buck's parents were familiar with the novel and chose to name her Pearl because of the value Hawthorne places on the young girl despite being born without knowing who the father was. I found this a fascinating connection between one great artist and another.

We spent about four hours at home before leaving for our next destination. I remember reading *The Good Earth,* and it is a great story, but I cannot say what else she wrote. She is different from what one can consider an American writer since her subject matter mainly deals with her extensive experiences in China. I never viewed her as an American writer and wondered about her fascination with China.

We next visited Philadelphia to see the Edgar Allan Poe National Historic Site. My fondness for Edgar Allan Poe earned me the nickname "Poe" from my students because I loved teaching him and had a mustache and a receding hairline that matched Poe's. I had a huge poster photo of Poe in my classroom, and when I stood next to it, we looked a lot alike, except for the eyes and nose. Poe had those dark, beady eyes and sanguine nose, while my eyes were brown and my nose fuller. It was always a moment of levity as the students would chide me about perhaps being a descendant of Poe. Each year, when I got a new group of juniors (I taught two classes of juniors and three classes of seniors each year), my students would ask me when we would read Poe so that they could rib me about being him. When one is a teacher in high school, one's reputation precedes you. Students came into my class happy, knowing I was not the brutal, punishing English teacher my two children had at University High School in Irvine. Over the years, when I met people at social events, the one teacher they had to complain about when they were in high school was the English teacher. I did not want to be that kind of English teacher. I wanted students to succeed, and I wanted them to have a good experience reading the most excellent English and American authors.

We arrived at the Poe National Historic Site in Philadelphia around mid-afternoon, just in time for a tour of the house that Poe had lived in. Poe never succeeded financially with the writings he did, so he was moving from one location to another with great regularity. During the tour, the national park ranger, who was very well-versed in his knowledge of Edgar Allan Poe, took us downstairs in the basement. While going down the steps, I noticed that the chimney was indented and a "pocket" existed in the brickwork. I told the tour, "This is where Poe probably wrote the short story "The Black Cat." The park ranger, unfamiliar with the story, said, "Why is that?" I told the tour that the story was about a man who hated his wife's black cat, and the couple fought over possession of the animal. One day, while trying to negotiate the steps down into the cellar, the black cat nearly tripped the husband, and he got so mad that he grabbed a hatchet to whack the cat when his wife intervened. Instead of whacking the cat, the husband whacks his wife over the head with the hatchet and buries her in the hole in the chimney. When the police come to investigate the screaming that the neighbors reported coming from the house, the husband takes them around to show that nothing is wrong. When they reach the cellar, the police hear a cat's meow behind the newly walled chimney. After tapping on the chimney, the police remove the newly placed bricks and find the cat sitting on the head of the wife, who has a hatchet buried in her head.

The floorboards in another part of the house were cracked, and one could tell they had been repaired. These floorboards are where the crazed man in the short story "The Tell-Tale Heart" buried the old man with the blue eye. The idea that the heart would continue to beat in the brain of the murderer was just a stroke of Poe's genius. One can imagine the story created in Poe's head as he walked the planks of this house, thinking of stories to write. He was highly imaginative and incredibly adept at telling stories.

I taught my students that Poe was the original detective and the first horror story writer. At the same time, "The Black Cat" was partly Poe's sense of humor to write a story like that. Another humorous Poe story I read to the students was "Hop-Frog." It was Poe at his most macabre and most humorous. The tour was fantastic, and I learned a few new things about Poe. We went outside and stood next to the giant stature of a Raven. Reading "The Raven" under this statue was supposed to be part of the experience of seeing this landmark. Reading "The Raven" was one of my favorite things when I taught Poe. Part of my persona as a teacher was creating the voices of the characters of the poems and stories we read. Although there was no voice to replicate in the poem, the repetitive utterance of "Nevermore" by the Raven is what charmed the students. In Poe's "The Fall of the House of Usher," the main character, Roderick Usher, is a strange guy with a very desperate voice. I created that voice for students, and all they could do was laugh. Making literature come alive was the goal of my teaching of literature. This is the house where Poe wrote the poem "The Raven." It made him famous, and all he got was sixteen dollars for the publication in a newspaper. I read the poem often but did not have time to do it at this house.

EDGAR ALLAN POE HOUSE IN PHILADELPHIA

Taking this tour is something I wished I had done before I started teaching. Those who teach American literature in the Eastern part of the country have a significant advantage over those who teach it out West. We just do not have a connection with the environment of those authors that many teachers back east have. I am glad to have been so engaged in teaching Poe. We are not done with Poe because we will see his gravesite in Baltimore and another house he lived in.

The successful teaching of American Literature required a visit to the surroundings of those authors. Allowing teachers to visit these historic homes of our best American authors brings them more to life for our students. Taking these trips used to be a tax write-off, but the geniuses in Washington thought that was not right and took away that benefit. Somehow, the exacting quote about Congress from Mark Twain comes to mind: "Suppose you were an idiot. Suppose you were a member of Congress. However, I repeat myself." Sadly, I am doing this visitation long after I retired from teaching in 2008. We stayed the night in Philadelphia, one of my favorite cities in the country, primarily because of their incredible pizza and cheesesteaks.

JUNE 6TH, 2014

The next day, we headed to Baltimore, Maryland, to visit the site of Poe's burial and another home where he resided. Poe was buried in Westminster Hall Church and Burying Ground twice. He was buried behind the church and moved to the front several years later. He has a large burial stone that beckons any visitor who admires Poe. Each year, starting in 1949, the one-hundredth anniversary of Poe's passing, a mysterious man with a large-brimmed hat and cloak comes to praise Poe by placing three red roses on his grave and a half-empty bottle of cognac. No one knows who the praiser of Poe is, but it appears that his name and mystery are forever finished because he has not shown up for the last ten years. He kept up the ritual for about fifty years.

**EDGAR ALLAN POE GRAVESTONE
IN BALTIMORE, MARYLAND**

I took pictures of the gravesite and spoke to Poe, telling him how great his stories were and how much my students enjoyed his sense of humor. We then headed down the street to see the home where he resided in Baltimore, and we found ourselves walking into a problematic neighborhood. We got to the house, which was closed because it was after two o'clock and the house was already locked. It was a scary walk back to the car and troubled me. Why do we have to worry about our safety in specific neighborhoods here in America? The idea that we are not free to walk where we want to walk is different from what I would call being free in America. Although I realize I could be in France and walk into the wrong neighborhood, it does not excuse the crass behavior of those in those neighborhoods. America is not necessarily the land of the free.

There has been much speculation about Poe's passing. He ended up in Washington Medical College for four days in total delirium. The medical research shows that a bat may have bitten him and that he suffered from delirium and the consequences of rabies. Sadly, he was only forty years old. Rest in peace, Edgar. I loved your work, and so did my students.

We went to lunch at The Horse You Came In On Saloon, supposedly where Poe got drunk for the last time. It is believed that this was the last place Edgar was seen before he ended up in the hospital. There is a seat in the bar marked Poe's Last Stop. Just across the way was another Poe accolade, Annabel Lee Tavern, a beautiful restaurant in honor of one of Poe's most famous poems, "Annabel Lee." We had lunch at the saloon, so we had to forgo the chance for dinner at the tavern, but it was just associated with Poe's poem and not with Poe himself.

Poe lived in New York City but moved to Fordham, New York, when his wife, Virginia Clemm, became ill with tuberculosis. He, Virginia, and her mother lived in a small white cottage to save Virginia. Sadly, she died there on January 30, 1847, and Poe became despondent. We wanted to see this cottage, but the time element was too challenging to get to the Bronx, so we did not go there. However, it is where Poe wrote the poem "Annabel Lee" that eulogized his wife, Virginia. The home still exists as a National Historic Landmark.

We then drove north to get to Tarrytown, New York. We got there late at night. The next day was all about Washington Irving.

JUNE 7TH, 2014

Washington Irving was one of the first significant fictional writers in American Literature. When I taught his work, I would be sure to teach it near the end of October because "The Legend of Sleepy Hollow" is one of my favorite all-time stories. The classic character of Ichabod Crane is one never to be forgotten. The following day, after a light breakfast, we went to Sunnyside, the longtime home of Washington Irving, and took a tour of his house. It is a beautiful Gothic Revival house on the banks of the Hudson River. Washington Irving expanded the original house; it has been restored to look much like it did in the 1850s.

ST. MARK'S EPISCOPAL CHURCH IN
SLEEPY HOLLOW, NEW YORK

The house's front entrance is draped in a wisteria vine that blooms in the spring and summer. It was in full, beautiful bloom when we got there. The view out the back at the Hudson River is something special—the vast river is considered incredible.   The house was beautiful and kept in the style of the 1850s when Irving lived there. The home is in a town called Irvington, named in honor of the author in 1854. We were told on the tour that his kitchen exceeded the quality of the kitchen at the White House. It was the most modern kitchen that could be for that period. Washington Irving lived quite a life for the 76 years he was around.

Washington Irving was the first American writer who earned money as a writer. He incorporated his excellent storytelling with the desire to entertain his reading audience. He was the first American fiction writer that gained great popularity. His non-fiction works were equally popular but less known than his famous short stories. I loved teaching three works of his: "The Legend of Sleepy Hollow," "Rip Van Winkle," and "The Devil and Tom Walker." The voices of Ichabod Crane, Rip Van Winkle, and Tom Walker were some of the more enjoyable "creations" of my teaching. After the final test on the unit of Washington Irving, we watched the Disney version of the story "The Legend of Sleepy Hollow." It was well done and quite enjoyable. We ate Halloween candy and laughed at the silliness of Ichabod Crane.

The house's interior was just incredible and had such a mixture of furniture that reflected the international person Washington Irving was. His desk and chair were something special for the period. He wrote his five-volume work on George Washington, whom he met at age six, in the study of this house, but his famous works were written in England during his seventeen-year stay there between 1825 and 1832. He was famous, knew several presidents, and entertained Charles Dickens and Sir Walter Scott at this home. In his work "The Life and Letters of Washington Irving," he wrote,

"Of all the scenery of the Hudson, the Kaatskill Mountains had the most witching effect on my boyish imagination."

Washington Irving was also famous for calling New York City "Gotham" (take that, Batman). It is an Anglo-Saxon word meaning "Goat's Town." Irving was famous for using pseudonyms, with Dieddrich Knickerbocker one of the more famous names used by the New York NBA team, the New York Knickerbockers. Another famous name he used was Geoffrey Crayon, the one he used to write his famous short stories, his original pseudonym.

After the house tour, we drove over to the Sleepy Hollow Cemetery and visited the gravesite of this famous American author. While there, we saw a flier indicating a cemetery walk at night with stories about the cemetery's inhabitants. We went that night and were thoroughly entertained by the stories of all the famous people buried at Sleepy Hollow Cemetery: Andrew Carnegie, Walter Chrysler, Samuel Gompers, Elizabeth Arden, Leona Helmsley, Brooke Astor, and William Rockefeller. It was a scary and spooky night, but we survived it.

JUNE 8, 2014

It was less than a two-hour drive to Hartford, Connecticut, where we wanted to see the house Mark Twain built and lived in during his most lucrative years. This was especially exciting because Mark Twain and William Shakespeare are my favorite authors. Had I the insight to understand what it took to be a Twain scholar, I would have pursued the endeavor. I loved the humor of Mark Twain. His insights into the human soul were as good as Shakespeare himself. When we arrived, we were just amazed at the beauty of the house he had built. We bought our tour tickets and waited for our time. In the meantime, we managed to see the house of one of his neighbors, Harriet Beecher Stowe, the author of *Uncle Tom's Cabin, 1852*. The book depicts the harsh conditions experienced by enslaved

African Americans. It was enormously popular and motivated the anti-slavery forces, angering those in the South. Over time, the issue of slavery became one of the driving forces that compelled our country into a civil war. It was a horrible war, and the consequences of it can be felt even in today's America.

Mark Twain's house was as magnificent as it looked from the outside. Every room was unique, and the bottom floor was constructed in mahogany. It was just stunning. Every room had its character and was decorated in Victorian style. The house was over eleven thousand square feet with twenty-five rooms. I do not recall exactly how many rooms we saw, but there were plenty to see. Twain named the house "Stormfield" after the short story "Captain Stormfield's Visit to Heaven." It was to be the family home for seventeen years, from 1873 to 1890. The library was a centerpiece of the house, given that people were entertained there with readings from his work and where Twain worked. For that period, a construction cost of $122,000 was an enormous sum for a house. They used Louis Comfort Tiffany and Associated Artists to paint the interior, which showed. They had Victorian interiors and remain one of the few left decorated in such spectacular fashion today. The house has ten thousand Victorian pieces, including a collection of Tiffany glass and rich holdings of Victorian housewares, decorative arts, and fine art. It was eye opening.

MARK TWAIN'S HOME IN HARTFORD, CONNECTICUT

Included in the house is the three-ton Paige typesetter that caused the financial ruin of Samuels Clemens. Twain had to sell the house to pay for the more than eighty thousand dollars in debt he had accumulated. He acquired that debt by perpetually putting money into the typesetting machine with over thirty thousand parts. The machine kept breaking down and never worked successfully. Twain chose to invest his money in this machine over the telephone. Literary artists could be better investors. To pay the debt, Twain and his wife traveled extensively to Europe to perform his works and entertain audiences in several countries. I understand that he made nearly two hundred thousand dollars during that extensive trip, enough to pay all his debts back and to live off for the rest of his life. He was a hard-working man.

Twain and his wife Livy had three daughters: Susy, Clara, and Jean. A son, Langdon, was born in 1870 but died in 1872. All the children would die young except for Clara, who became the sole heir of the Twain legacy. The loss of his children was the foundation of Twain's bitterness, and during the final years of his life, his literature reflected that bitterness. However, during the period they lived there, he managed to write *The Adventures of Tom Sawyer, A Tramp Abroad, The Prince and the Pauper, Life on the Mississippi, The Adventures of Huckleberry Finn,* and *A Connecticut Yankee in King Arthur's Court.* He wrote much of these works on the house's third floor, where his billiard table resided. When he took a break from writing, he played billiards. He also wrote at his wife's sister's house in Elmira, New York, where they spent the summers. We will be ending this literary trip in Elmira.

Twain was a humorist and a satirist, using humor to mock things he thought wrong. That is personally one of the primary reasons why I like him. He stood up against all odds and voiced his opinion on all matters. On my way home to California, I will visit the boyhood home of Mark Twain. Before that, we headed north to see the home of Herman Melville, the author of *Moby Dick.*

We arrived mid-afternoon in Pittsfield, Massachusetts, where Herman Melville's home, Arrowhead, resided. We arrived just in time for the last tour of his house and grounds for the day. This is where he wrote *Moby Dick,* but the critics did not receive the book well, even though his earlier works earned him a decent amount of money. Nathaniel Hawthorne, a mentor of Melville's, could see the beauty in the book, but literary praise for the book would not happen for thirty years after his death. Because of the financial failure of the book, Melville was forced to move his family to New York.

The home at Arrowhead was simple and was nothing close to the extraordinary home of Twain. Of note were Melville's writing room, a large table and the tools the author used while writing, an ink pot and blotter, long white quill pens, and a penknife for sharpening. Melville, as I already indicated, was the literary friend of Nathaniel Hawthorne, and both spent a great deal of time together. Melville, one might say, was taught literature by Hawthorne. Hawthorne was a writer who used symbols in his works, and Melville would catch on to the significant role of symbols when he wrote *Moby Dick*.

The book is dedicated to Nathaniel Hawthorne. When I learned this at Arrowhead, I realized I had spent my entire career as a teacher not knowing this. If I did, it would not matter to my students because of the distance from these authors, both mentally and physically.

HERMAN MELVILLE'S HOME IN PITTSFIELD, MASSACHUSETTS

Although I prided myself on my knowledge of the best writers in American literature, I held only a master's degree in the subject. It is tough to be knowledgeable about all American literature authors. To thoroughly know an author, one has to have read a biography of them. Let me shed some light on what an English teacher can know by demonstrating this with a college experience I had.

I recall when I was taking a graduate seminar in Ernest Hemingway, a substitute professor came into the room for our professor, and she confessed that she did not know much about the canon of work of Ernest Hemingway. Once an English and American literature master's degree is earned, students will focus on an English or American literature era. For example, if I had chosen to earn a Ph.D. in literature, I would have made Mark Twain the focus of my dissertation. In short, I would spend all my time reading the works of Twain to discover what I wanted to write about for my dissertation. A dissertation is a book written to prove a subject about the author's writings. I could argue that Twain was well-versed in the Bible and then begin to show how he used the Bible in his books. I imagine that would be easier if I were a Melwerele scholar because Melville constantly used Biblical passages and names in his works, especially *Moby Dick*. He also used Shakespeare as well. So, when a substitute professor does not know much about an author, it is because their concentration is on another author. Becoming an expert on an author requires the student to learn about the author's life, the works they wrote, and the intended meaning of each. If the author wrote extensively, the students were saddled with reading all of their works to gain competency in the canon of writings.

When the internet became available as a teacher, I would spend several hours learning about the life and writings of the authors I taught. Before the internet, it was much more challenging to learn about an author's life unless one read either a biography or autobiography of the same. Learning about all the authors in American and British literature was a vast undertaking. It took years for me to gain competence and understanding of these authors' places in literary history.

Although our stay at Arrowhead was short, a visit gave me a sense of what discipline Herman Melville had to write the book *Moby Dick*. To learn of his relationship with Hawthorne was terrific as well. I did not know of Hawthorne living in Lennox, Massachusetts, just a stone's throw from where Melville lived. Hawthorne was a long way from Salem, Massachusetts, a stop we have yet to reach.

JUNE 9, 2014

After a long leisurely breakfast, we left for Lennox, Massachusetts, to see the house of Edith Wharton called The Mount, which was just a fifteen-minute drive from Pittsfield and Lennox, where Hawthorne lived. Hawthorne could not pay his rent on the Salem house, so they moved to a small cottage in Lennox. It was an immaterial place to see because it no longer existed. It is, however, where he wrote *The House of the Seven Gables*, published in 1851. The Lennox cottage was a rental property that did not convert to a site to visit since Hawthorne was not there that long.

Tours for Edith Wharton's house did not start until ten o'clock, so there was no hurry to get there early, or at least we did not think so. When we arrived, we could not believe the extensive grounds and the huge house we discovered. It testified to how different authors thrived in those days with monetary success from selling their books. Edith Wharton hit the jackpot. The house was undoubtedly the most beautiful of all the authors we had seen so far and by a long shot.

EDITH WHARTON HOUSE IN LENNOX, MASSACHUSETTS

When I was a sophomore in high school, we read *Ethan Frome,* the novel of Whaton's that was somehow manageable for fifteen-year-olds. I did not relate to the novel or the story. What can a fifteen-year-old bring to a novel of an older man with an invalid wife who falls in love with his young housemaid? This is a testimony to the random choices of reading we did in the early 1960s. I suppose the idea was to expose us to great literature, and for that, I am grateful, but Wharton's vocabulary was unsuitable for the high school sophomore reader. Allowing students to read novels way beyond their reading vocabulary levels is absurd, an argument I have often made as an English teacher. I have preliminary work on a book that argues this position: too many of the literary works are too far above the reading level of most students.

A book's readability is essential to a reader's language growth. Reading literary works is impossible if the reading material is three or four grade levels above the student's reading level. It may be possible, but not productive. It is punitive to make students read books that exceed their reading levels. *Great Expectations* is not a book for first-year students in high school. The word paid Charles Dickens, so he used his "best" vocabulary when writing his novels. Reading his works became an arduous task for students with a limited vocabulary. Many novels are readable and suitable for high school students. When I was in high school, I found my comfort level in reading the novels of John Steinbeck, and I read twelve of his novels in one year, walking from one classroom to the next. I read a great deal in my chemistry class alone. The reader will have to read my book about literature to understand why I could read so many books in my chemistry class.

After three hours of visiting The Mount, we headed to Amherst to visit the home of Emily Dickinson. The drive from Lennox to Amherst was both beautiful and short. We could not wait to see her house. We arrived at Emily Dickinson Homestead in the early afternoon and entered the day's first-afternoon tour. Walking into the house was an experience in itself. It was a charming house and a place almost anyone would want to grow up in. Emily lived forty of her fifty-five years at this house. While living there, she managed to write over eighteen hundred poems, of which only ten were published in her lifetime. She did not want the recognition, and she prized her lack of fame. She knew she would be famous if she allowed her poetry to be published as it was written, but instead kept them in a dresser drawer until she passed away and her sister-in-law took the time to organize and publish them. Emily was the original "closet" poet.

One time, in an interview for a college job, I was asked if I wrote poetry, and my answer was, "Yes, they are safely tucked away in a dresser drawer." I tried to be funny, and some committee members laughed. The reality was that my poetry had been hiding in my computer for many years, and I never dared to publish any of them, but I plan to publish all of them before I leave this earth forever. I will not topple the poetic world with them, and perhaps none of them are worth a hoot, but I think there might be a couple with some merit. I will leave that to the critics.

Inside this beautiful home, we learned of the daily life of Emily. She was an all-around goodie with two shoes. She cooked, she baked, she sewed, she was a gardener, a poet, and a letter writer. Her legacy was left in her words through her letters and poetry. She did most of her writing at her desk in her bedroom. However, she wrote in the kitchen and elsewhere in the house whenever the poetic inspiration occurred. A poet is always working on another poem.

The house was designated a National Historic Landmark in 1964 and purchased by the Trustees of Amherst College. The house has a one-and-a-half-acre garden that features a variety of flowers and plants. Many of these were referred to in the poetry of Dickinson. She summed up her life with the following poem:

This is my letter to the world
That never wrote to Me—-
The simple News is that Nature
told—
With tender Majesty.

Her Message is committed
To Hands I cannot see–
For love of Her–Sweet-
countrymen—
Judge tenderly—of Me.

She wrote about the natural world around her, questioned the existence of God, and delved into the nature of the human soul. Emily was America's greatest female poet. She combined a modern writing style with genius insights into her nature and the natural world.

After the tour, we went to Amherst College and considered it one of the prettiest colleges we had ever seen. One of the side tours during this trip was to visit the college campuses that were famous nearby. Amherst is just a beautiful liberal arts college. I cannot imagine a more idyllic place to go to college. We learned of Emily going to college and that her father was entirely involved with the original establishment of this extraordinary learning institution. Dickinson's grandfather, Samuel Fowler Dickinson, was one of the college's founders; her father, Edward Dickinson, was college treasurer from 1835 to 1873; her brother William Austin Dickinson took over as treasurer from 1873 until 1895. The Dickinson family and Amherst are synonymous. Noah Webster was the founder of Amherst College. The college is named after Lord Jeffrey Amherst, a colonial-era military hero.

JUNE 10, 2014

Our next stop was to Concord, Massachusetts. Concord would require a few days to explore since we have Ralph Waldo Emerson, Nathaniel Hawthorne, Louisa May Alcott, and Henry David Thoreau in the same area. We started with the house of Nathaniel Hawthorne. Although Hawthorne lived in Lennox, he managed to move around like most starving artists. There was no historic site for Hawthorne in Lennox and not even an address to explore, so those living in residence were not constantly badgered about the goings on of Hawthorne. So we found the house he and Emerson had lived in for different periods. The Old Manse was the home of both at once and was located in Concord.

Hawthorne was the author who wrote for ten years and then decided to burn all of his writings before he published his first book, *Fanshawe, in 1828.* He was one of the originators of the short story. He and his wife, Sophia, moved into the house on their wedding day on July 9, 1842. They would reside in Concord for three years. In front of the house is an extensive garden, and Hawthorne's friend, Henry David Thoreau, built it as a wedding gift. It was an incredible garden. It was pretty extensive and probably fed the Hawthorns for the entire winter.

Hawthorne changed his name from Hathorne by adding the "w" to escape the association with the Hathorne's of the Salem Witch Trials. The Hathorne's were Nathaniel's ancestors and the irony is that Nathaniel would write one of the greatest works about the Puritans of New England, *The Scarlet Letter.* The novel was published in 1850, so many years of practice existed before his masterpiece was published. While at the Old Manse, Hawthorne wrote short stories and published them in a book called *Mosses from an Old Manse. "Rappacinni's Daughter" and "The Birthmark"* were two stories he wrote while there. When I taught Hawthorne, I used to call him Mr. Ambiguity. I called him that because he always left the reader to determine the meaning of the short stories he wrote. Students would struggle for his intended meaning for any of the stories we read, like "Dr. Heidegger's Experiment."

I recall the writing room where Hawthorne wrote. It was on the house's second floor, and the small desk he wrote on was so tiny that it was remarkable that anyone would have the concentration to write is such a small space. It faced the wall so he would not be distracted by looking out the windows where one could see the beautiful landscape. Hawthorne was highly disciplined. We have another stop for Hawthorne, so I will stop now and continue with him when we get to Salem, Massachusetts, where he was born and lived for several years.

The Ralph Waldo Emerson Memorial House, a Colonial architecture, was less than a mile from the Old Manse. It is a National Historic Landmark. Emerson and his family moved into the house when he was thirty-two, and he spent fifty years there, passing away in 1882. Emerson founded the Transcendental Movement, which dominated the thinking at the time. They were the hippies of the 1850s. The movement focused on the respect and reverence for nature.

Emerson also owned forty acres of land near Walden Pond, where his comrade Henry David Thoreau would build his cabin. Henry was a friend of Waldo's and even lived at his house for some time. Incredibly, Henry never established a place he could call his own except for the cabin he built in the woods and was there for less than two years. I will reserve more discussion of Thoreau until we go out and visit the small cabin he built near Walden Pond. Emerson's children enjoyed their walks with their father in Walden Woods.

Teaching Emerson was no joy since much of his writing flew over the heads of 16-year-old juniors. The honors students even struggled with his language. I realized that teaching American Literature to juniors in high school was more about teaching cultural literacy than improving their literacy. How can one's literacy improve when one is teaching Emerson? Where was the connection if Emerson's language superseded the students' language? What was the point? I could argue just one thing: that students were becoming culturally more literate but not better readers or writers.

Learning about the authors of American literature was designed to make the students aware of the best writers in American history. I often had to make that argument when I taught several authors because literacy was not the goal of reading authors whose language levels far exceeded the readers in my class, but cultural literacy was the goal. Students could say they knew who American literature's influential writers were.

When students walked into class on the first day, I asked them to write down all the authors they knew who were American writers. Charles Dickens was a standard answer. William Shakespeare even got the nod from some students. Literature for students at the first and second-year student levels of high school was a mixture of American, English, and world literature. It confused students because teachers needed to segregate the authors and their countries. Naturally, when students read the works of those authors, most English teachers did not distinguish whether one was American, English, or German. They just read the stories, the poems, and essays—the author was secondary, if that. So they would waltz into American literature, ignorant of who wrote the story and what country they were from: England, America, or some European country. Emerson's house was beautiful, and his library magnificent. After lunch, we drove down the street to see the Louisa May Alcott Orchard House. This was a house that was as simple as it gets. Bronson Allcott and his wife, Abigail, lived at this residence for about twenty years. It is here where Louisa May wrote her famous novel *Little Women*. Each of the four children was depicted in the novel with fictional names, and Louisa captured the family's lifestyle in those days. The area surrounding them was twelve acres with two large apple orchards.

Bronson was an outspoken leader in educational reform and often had Thoreau, Emerson, and Hawthorne as guests at the house for philosophical discussions. It would have been interesting to hear what they had to say, and I imagined being a fly on the wall listening to these intellectual men speak about education. Harvard was already two hundred years old as an institution, and both Emerson and Thoreau were graduates. Although not as formerly educated, Bronson was self-educated, a progressive advocate for women's rights, and an abolitionist.

The day was done, and our heads were spinning with facts, so I spent the time writing down as much as I could remember. Tomorrow would be a trip to Walden Pond, a place I had always wanted to see.

JUNE 11–12, 2014

Walden Pond is but a mile and a half from the Emerson house, and Henry David Thoreau was living at their house when he built his famous little house in the woods of Walden Pond. It took Henry, with the help of friends, to finish the cabin in about three months. The year was 1845. His famous words that indicated the reason for building the little house were: "I went to the woods because I wished to live deliberately, to front only the essential facts of life, and see if I could not learn what it had to teach and not, when I came to die, discover that I had not lived (Walden 69). Thus, he lived there for two years, two months, and two days. In Thoreau's time there was an effort to live with self-sufficiency and exercise some introspection. Thoreau spent his days reading, writing, and exploring the woods. He lived close to nature and "sucked out all the marrow of it," as he put it. He lived there from July 4, 1845, to

September 6, 1847. Out of that experience came the book *Walden, or Life in the Woods.*

Thoreau lived and observed and wrote his observations in journals that he kept for the time he lived there. He then condensed the two years into one and revised his work several times before publishing it. In the book, he advocated living simply and argued that buying a farm ties one down to a responsibility he did not want to have. We should spend our time living in concert with nature, and our lives would be much more fulfilled. He was a Transcendentalist like Emerson. I thought there were the hippies of the 1850s. I compared them to the hippies of the 1960s. He felt that this was living and that other distractions take from the process of living deliberately. The question he pursued was to determine what the meaning of life is. Should we spend our time pursuing riches, or what should we be doing?

I thought of a speech I had heard by Steven Jobs at a Stanford commencement. I believe it has value here when juxtaposed with the life of Henry David Thoreau:

I am honored to be with you today at your commencement from one of the finest universities in the world. I never graduated from college. This is the closest I've ever gotten to a college graduation. Today, I want to tell you three stories from my life. That's it. No big deal. Just three stories.

The first story is about connecting the dots.

I dropped out of Reed College after the first six months but then stayed around as a drop-in for another 18 months or so before I quit. So why did I drop out? It started before I was born. My biological mother was a young, unwed college graduate student, and she decided to put me up for adoption. She felt strongly that college graduates should adopt me, so everything was all set for me to be adopted at birth by a lawyer and his wife. Except that when I popped out, they decided at the last minute that they wanted a girl. So my parents, on a waiting list, got a call in the middle of the night asking: "We have an unexpected baby boy; do you want him?" They said: "Of course." My biological mother later found out that my mother had never graduated from college and that my father had never graduated from high school. She relented a few months later when my parents said I would attend college. But I naively chose a college almost as expensive as Stanford, and all of my working-class parents' savings were being spent on my college tuition.

After six months, I couldn't see the value in it. I had no idea what I wanted to do with my life and no idea how college was going to help me figure that out. And here I was, spending all of the money my parents had saved their entire life. So I decided to drop out and trust that it would all work out OK. It was pretty scary at the time, but looking back, it was one of the best decisions I ever made. The minute I dropped out, I could stop taking the required classes that didn't interest me and begin dropping in on the ones that looked interesting.

It wasn't all romantic. I didn't have a dorm room, so I slept on the floor in a friend's room. I returned Coke bottles for the 5-cent deposits to buy food with, and I would walk the 7 miles across town every Saturday to get one good meal a week at the Harne Krishna temple. I loved it. And much of what I stumbled into by following my curiosity and intuition turned out to be priceless later on. Let me give you an example.

Reed College at that time offered perhaps the best calligraphy instruction in the country. Throughout the campus every poster, every label on every drawer, was beautifully hand calligraphed. Because I had dropped out and didn't have to take normal classes, I decided to take a calligraphy class to learn how to do this. I learned about serif, and sans serif typefaces, about varying the amount of space between different letter combinations, about what makes great typography great. It was beautiful, historical, and artistically subtle in a way that science can't capture, and I found it fascinating.

None of this had even a hope of any practical application in my life. But 10 years later, when we were designing the first Macintosh computer, it all came back to me. And we designed it all for the Mac. It was the first computer with beautiful typography. If I had never dropped in on that single course in college, the Mac would have never had multiple typefaces or proportionally spaced fonts. And since Windows just copied the Mac, it's likely that no personal computer would have them. If I had never dropped out, I would have never dropped in on this calligraphy class, and personal computers might not have the wonderful typography that they do. Of course, it was impossible to connect the dots looking forward when I was in college. But it was very, very clear looking back 10 years later.

Again, you can't connect the dots looking forward; you can only connect them looking backward. So, you have to trust that the dots will somehow connect in your future. You have to trust in something—your gut, destiny, life, karma, whatever. This approach has never let me down, and it has made all the difference in my life.

My second story is about love and loss.

I was lucky—I found what I loved to do early in life. Woz and I started Apple in my parents' garage when I was twenty. We worked hard, and in 10 years, Apple had grown from just the two of us in a garage into a 2 billion company with over 4,000 employees. We had just released our finest creation–the Macintosh—a year earlier, and I had just turned 3. And then I got fired. How can you get fired from a company you started? Well, as Apple grew we hired someone who I thought was very talented to run the company with me, and for the first year or so things went well. But then our visions of the future began to diverge and eventually, we had a falling out. When we did, our Board of Directors sided with him. So, at 30, I was out. And very publically out. What had been the focus of my entire adult life was gone, and it was devastating.

I really didn't know what to do for the next few months. I felt that I had let the previous generation of entrepreneurs down—that I had dropped the baton as it was being passed to me. I met with David Packard and Bob Noyce and tried to apologize for screwing up so badly. I was a very public failure, and I even thought about running away from the valley. But something slowly began to dawn on me—I still loved what I did. I had been rejected, but I was still in love. And so I decided to start over.

I didn't see it then, but it turned out getting fired by Apple was the best thing that could have ever happened to me. The heaviness of being successful was replaced by the lightness of being a beginner again, less sure about everything. It freed me to enter one of the most creative periods of my life.

During the next five years, I started a company named MeXT, and another company named Pixar, and fell in love with an amazing woman who would become my wife. Pixar went on to create the world's first computer animated feature film, Toy Story and is now the most successful animation studio in the world. In a remarkable turn of events, Apple bought NeXT, I returned to Apple, and the technology we developed at NeXT is at the heart of Apple's current renaissance. And Larene and I have a wonderful family together.

I'm pretty sure none of this would have happened if I hadn't been fired from Apple. It was awful-tasting medicine, but I guess the patient needed it. Sometimes life hits you in the head with a brick. Don't lose faith. I'm convinced that the only thing that kept me going was that I loved what I did. You've got to find what you love. And that is as true for your work as it is for your lovers. Your work is going to fill a large part of your life and the only way to do great work is to love what you do. If you haven't found it yet, keep looking. Don't settle. As with all matters of the heart, you'll know when you find it. And, like any great relationship, it just gets better and better as the years roll on. So keep looking until you find it. Don't settle.

My third story is about death.

When I was 17, I read a quote that went something like: "If you live each day as if it was your last, someday you most certainly will be right." It made an impression on me, and since then, for the past 33 years, I have looked in the mirror every morning and asked myself: "If today were the last day of my life, would I want to do what I am about to do today?" And whenever the answer has been "No" for too many days in a row, I know I need to change something.

Remembering that I'll be dead soon is the most important tool I've ever encountered to help me make the big choices in life. Because almost everything–all external expectations, all pride, all fear of embarrassment or failure—these things just fall away in the face of death, leaving only what is truly important. Remembering that you are going to die is the best way I know to avoid the trap of thinking you have something to lose. You are already naked. There is no reason not to follow your heart.

About a year ago, I was diagnosed with cancer. I had a scan at 7:30 in the morning, and it clearly showed a tumor on my pancreas. I didn't even know what a pancreas was. The doctors told me that it was almost certainly a type of cancer that was incurable and that I should expect to live no longer than three to six months. My doctor advised me to go home and get my affairs in order, which is the doctor's code for preparing to die. It means to try to tell your kids everything you thought you'd have the next ten years to tell them in just a few months. It means to make sure everything is buttoned up so that it will be as easy as possible for your family. It means to say your goodbyes.

I lived with that diagnosis all day. Later that evening, I had a biopsy, where they stuck an endoscope down my throat, through my stomach, and into my intestines, put a needle into my pancreas, and got a few cells from the tumor. I was sedated, but my wife, who was there, told me that when they viewed the cells under a microscope, the doctors started crying because it turned out to be a very rare form of pancreatic cancer that is curable with surgery. I had the surgery, and I'm fine now.

That was the closest I've been to facing death, and I hope it's the closest I get for a few more decades. Having lived through it, I can now say this to you with a bit more certainty than when death was a useful but purely intellectual concept.

No one wants to die. Even people who want to go to heaven don't want to die to get there. And yet death is the destination we will all share. No one has ever escaped it. And that is as it should be, because Death is, very likely, the single best invention in life. It is Life's change agent. It clears out the old to make way for the new. Right now the new is you, but someday, not too long from now, you will gradually become the old and be cleared away. Sorry to be so dramatic, but it is quite true.

Your time is limited, so don't waste it living someone else's life. Don't be trapped by dogma—which is living with the results of other people's thinking. Don't let the noise of other's opinions drown out your own inner voice. And most importantly, have the courage to follow your heart and intuition. They somehow already know what you truly want to become. Everything else is secondary.

When I was young, there was an amazing publication called The Whole Earth Catalog, which was one of the Bibles of my generation. It was created by a fellow named Stewart Brand not far from here in Menlo Park, and he brought it to life with his poetic touch. This was in the late 1960s, before personal computers and desktop publishing, so it was all made with typewriters, scissors, and Polaroid cameras. It was sort of like Google in paperback form, 35 years before Google came along: it was idealistic and overflowing with neat tools and great notions.

Stewart and his team put out several issues of The Whole Earth Catalog, and then when it had run its course, they put out a final issue. It was the mid-1970s, and I was your age. On the back cover of their final issue was a photograph of an early morning country road, the kind you find yourself hitchhiking on if you were so adventurous. Beneath it were the words: "Stay Hungry. Stay Foolish." It was their farewell message as they signed off. Stay Hungry. Stay Foolish. And I have always wished that for myself. And now, as you graduate to begin anew, I wish that for you. Stay Hungry, Stay Foolish.

Thank you all very much,

Steven Jobs

Steven Jobs found what he loved to do in life, and he pursued it with a passion. The results were fabulous. Given that we have a meager amount of time in life to accomplish something, we all want to make our mark on the world. The mark I attempted to make was to impress students with the beauty and value of literature. I loved literature, and I loved teaching it. There was always a big disconnect between the literature and the students at the high school level because they were so young and could not bring the experiences necessary to identify with the likes of Thoreau, Emerson, and Dickenson. But I tried to connect them to the literature and give them some cultural literacy, an awareness of those great authors of American Literature.

Jobs also understood that his time on earth was finite and that everything must pass. One generation comes as another goes, and so the sun also rises on a new generation. It would be just six years later that Jobs would pass away. It was just a jot of time. I am seventy-five at the time of this writing, and I know my time is limited, but I have promised to keep but not miles to go before I sleep.

As we continued to walk to find the site where the cabin of Thoreau had been, I thought how lovely this setting was. I thought of the line from Robert Frost's poem "Stopping by Woods." "The woods are lovely, dark and deep…" I could not help but think how much more I could have brought to the learning table had I visited this site before teaching my students. A teacher's education never stops and should be bolstered with travel, and promoting that travel will help bring the places where these authors resided to life in the classroom. Mark Twain said, "Travel is fatal to bigotry and narrow-mindedness, and many people need it sorely on these accounts. Broad, wholesome, charitable views of men and things cannot be acquired by vegetating in one little corner of the earth all one's lifetime." Perhaps I am traveling too late in life, but since learning should be something one does for an entire lifetime, I continue to learn as long as I have a life.

It was a beautiful walk along the lake of Walden Pond and a beautiful afternoon. I imagined Henry sitting in his rowboat, fishing. He said, "Time is but a stream I go fishing in..." and all his philosophical wonder came to me.

JUNE 13, 2014

The following day, we found ourselves at the door of a former residence of Robert Frost when he taught at Harvard. It was not a place to visit, but it had a historical marker near the door to tell us about his presence there. We stumbled on it while walking to the campus to see what the great Harvard University was like. It did not disappoint. It was an incredible campus and the most iconic Ivy League school of the family. Students had already gone home for the summer, but the ambitious were there taking summer school classes, but it needed to be teeming with students. The ivy walls, beautiful brick buildings, and gorgeous libraries were there.

It was a massive campus that would take hours to circum-navigate, so instead of doing that, we went to the house of Henry Wadsworth Longfellow, poet laureate.

"Listen, my children, and you shall hear of the midnight ride of Paul Revere." Longfellow was a famous American poet who hit the big time marrying Fannie Appleton, whose father bought the house as their wedding gift. The house was almost as inspiring as Edith Wharton's, for it was exquisite. The library and study of Longfellow was one that only dreams are made of. I loved the twenty-five-room house on two acres of land in Cambridge. The house was a mid-Georgian Colonial and is considered one of America's finest historic homes.

Longfellow's popularity as a poet had students reciting his poetry in school for decades. He was considered to be America's finest poet of his period. His style was more classic, with stanzas, rhymes, and cadences, allowing anyone to memorize and recite easily. He was the first poet actually to make a living writing poetry. Longfellow attended Bowdoin College from 1821-1825 when he was fourteen. Some of his classmates were Nathaniel Hawthorne and Franklin Pierce. Each would maintain a friendship their entire lives. All three graduated about the same time.

Longfellow was born one of eight children in Portland, Maine, and his birthplace house is a National Historic Site. He was very fond of the house he shared with his eight brothers and sisters, one of whom willed the home to the National Historical Society. Longfellow penned several poems at the Portland residence and often visited the home until he died in 1882. He enjoyed the home and wrote several poems commemorating his memories at that residence. The gardens behind the home are said to contain flowers blooming there since the early 19th century. We did not go as far as Maine to see this house on this literary trip, and my knowledge comes from a book about his life at that residence. However, his Cambridge home was incredible and beyond the means of a professor of language at Harvard. The house was kept in the family for many years after his passing in 1882 and turned over to the National Park Service in 1972.

JUNE 14, 2014

From Cambridge, we drove to Salem to see another famous house, the birthplace residence of Nathaniel Hawthorne. The original house where Hawthorne was born was moved to the site of The House of the Seven Gables. When Hawthorne was young, he visited his cousin at this house and eventually used it as material for the novel of the same name. The birthplace home was simple, with three rooms on the first and three on the second floors, unremarkable. The Seven Gables house was quite a home with a secret stairway from the first floor to the third floor. Walking up the spiraling staircase to the house's third floor was interesting, while missing the second floor on the way up. It was a memorable experience. No one quite knew the reason for its existence, and the tour guide left it a mystery. We made it to the top without passing out.

Hawthorne worked at the Salem Custom House for three years to earn money to support his family. During that time, he discovered a torn cloth in the attic of the custom house with the embroidered letter "A" on it, and it set his imagination to conceive the novel *The Scarlet Letter,* perhaps the most beautifully written novel in American Literature. After completing the Salem Custom House job, he wrote the novel *The Scarlet Letter,* then moved to Lennox, where he would write The House of the Seven Gables and fraternize with Melville, as I already mentioned. As the reader may recall, he worked with Herman Melville on the novel *Moby Dick*, but it took many years before it was recognized as a great book. Hawthorne, however, enjoyed more success but not much more: *The Scarlet Letter* sold about 7800 copies in Hawthorne's lifetime, but not enough to make him rich.

Thus, we have come full circle with Hawthorne, and we are finally done learning all we can about this famous author. What was significant about his writing of the novel was important to me. Hawthorne left a commentary on his ancestry. This is a book on ancestry and finding my roots. Hawthorne was doing the same with *The Scarlet Letter.* "His family's history and association inspired Hawthorne with Puritan New England, and much of his work is set in 17th-century New England. Hawthorne, like many other Romantics, was also inspired by nature and the idea of the supernatural, as evidenced in his short story "Young Goodman Brown." (Cram.com)

Learning about my family's history inspired me to write this book. I wanted to share the family history with all my cousins and share the truth of what I found. Hawthorne was trying to shed some truth on the behavior of Puritan New England and his ancestors who were a significant part of the Salem Witch Trials of 1690. The irony of publicly chastising a woman for committing adultery when everyone in the town was a sinner of one sort or another. Hawthorne condemns the townspeople for their hypocrisy, a theme he carries throughout the book to demonstrate that about his ancestors. Those who have come before us are what we are today.

We left Salem to go to Derry, New Hampshire, and visit the first home of Robert Frost. The Frost Farm is a Historic House Museum where Frost lived from 1900 to 1911. His earlier life was spent in Laurence, Massachusetts, where he graduated high school in 1892. He married his high school sweetheart, Elinor Miriam White, with whom he shared valedictorian honors. She was also the central inspiration for his poetry. They had six children together. Tragically, Frost survived four of his six children, outlived his wife, and had a son die to suicide, and one of his daughters committed to a mental hospital. Frost began writing some of his more significant poems at the house in Derry. The house was quite nice inside and was a pleasant place, but it was kept as a museum because Frost lived there, wrote poetry, and raised chickens. He worked from dawn to dusk. The family lived there for eleven years, from 1900-1911. Shortly after that, they left for England because American magazines continuously rejected their poetry of Frost.

In England, he published two books of poetry, *A Boy's Will* and *North of Boston*, in 1913 and 1914, respectively. They were well received in English, and Frost and his family returned to the United States, and he was a recognized poet. Upon their return, they bought a home in Franconia, New Hampshire, from 1915 to 1920. This is the home where he wrote "The Road Not Taken" and "Stopping by Woods on a Snowy Evening," published in his next book, *Mountain Interval*. We drove from Derry to Franconia and got there too late to see the inside of the house, but we managed to walk the grounds a bit and see another of his abodes. While living here, Frost began teaching at Amherst College, and it would remain their summer home until 1936.

THE FROST PLACE IN FRANCONIA, NEW HAMPSHIRE

Finally, we drove to Bennington, where we spent an hour or so visiting the gravesite of Frost and his wife. His gravesite was on a hill overlooking the valley, and Frost would have a view of the nature he so dearly loved for as long as he rested here. Before his death, he spent twenty-four years in Ripton, Vermont, where he had a summer cabin, and spent time teaching at Middlebury College. Frost also taught at Dartmouth and Harvard during his illustrious career. I cannot help but reflect on the poem "The Road Not Taken" and its significance to Frost. He took the road less traveled, and that made all the difference.

JUNE 15, 2014

We drove from Bennington, Vermont, to Elmira, New York, to visit the summer home and gravesite of Mark Twain. The drive to Elmira was three and a half hours and one of the longer drives of the trip, but this would be the last author for this literary tour, and we saved the best for last. I say the best because Twain was one of a kind. We went to Elmira College because the little lookout room where he wrote *Huckleberry Finn* was on campus. We discovered all kinds of things to see about Twain. There was a statue in his honor on the campus, and materials in the college library featured Twain. Walking the campus at Elmira College was incredible, for I believe it to be the most beautiful campus in the country, even though I have not seen them all. It was undoubtedly one of the prettiest things we encountered in our travels, better than Harvard and Yale. We took pictures of his statue and sat on one of the pedestals that make up the monument.

MARK TWAIN'S WRITING HOUSE IN ELMIRA, NEW YORK

Mark Twain's importance as a writer was best described by Ernest Hemingway in his book *Green Hills of Africa* (1935) when he said, "All modern literature comes from one book by Mark Twain called *Huckleberry Finn.*" The novel uses a first-person narrator, Huck Finn, through whose eyes we see the American Society of the mid-19th century. The novel takes place in the 1840s, long before the emancipation of the black man in our society, long before the Civil War that was fought for the freedom of African Americans. Another writer, William Dean Howells, called Twain "the Lincoln of our Literature." Twain set free the idea that a twelve-year-old boy could tell a story. More importantly, the story is about the sensitive topic of racism in our society. The book does not end tragically but happily, so we must consider it a comedy instead of a tragedy. Twain's humor in the novel is quite apparent to those who see his satire on Southern Society. We see different dialects in the novel and people speaking like ordinary people in their region. This was the genius of Twain.

MARK TWAIN'S GRAVESTONE AT WOODLAWN CEMETARY IN ELMIRA, NEW YORK

When we visited the gravesite, it was unremarkable for a man of such stature, but Twain was humble and would approve. He said, "I am indifferent to going to heaven or hell since I have friends in both places." When I continue my trip out west, I will stop at the boyhood home of Twain in Hannibal, Missouri. Our next trip in August will be a historic trip to sacred historical sites in American history.

For now, we returned home to Hellertown, Pennsylvania, in less than three hours. We went to work on Nancy's Thoreauvian Garden.

RICHARD P. SINAY

NANCY'S THOREAUVIAN GARDEN IN
HELLERTOWN, PENNSYLVANIA

PART 5

BOSTON, MASSACHUSETTS TO GETTYSBURG, PENNSYLVANIA

JULY 30, 31, AND AUGUST 1, 2014

We flew to Boston to start our historic trip, and after renting a car, we drove to Boston to see the historical sites there. Although we had been here just last month, we were on a different mission: what could we learn about the American colonial era and the beginnings of our country? We drove to the Old North Church, where the lanterns were hung to warn the Patriots that the British were coming. One lantern meant they were coming by land, and two lanterns meant they were coming by sea.

I have to tell a story that is a comic side note. Once, in a meeting of junior English teachers, we were working on a Revolutionary Literature Unit to teach the students the literature at the time of the American Revolution. One of our group's teachers asked, "How did the British get to America?" and my response was, jokingly, that they flew into Boston. She said, "They did?" She seriously thought they had taken a plane. If any academic teacher does not have a master's degree in the subject area at the high school level, they should not be able to teach students at the junior and senior levels. I say this because the teacher needs to be smarter than the students.

If one cannot earn an academic master's, teachers have no business teaching juniors and seniors in high school.

To say that Boston is a historic town is an understatement: The Boston Tea Party and The Boston Massacre, along with the infamous Paul Revere, the Old North Church, the Old South Meeting House, and a lot of other important meetings around the time of The Revolutionary War in America. The Boston Tea Party was held because the colonials were tired of the taxes imposed on them by King George III. So the colonials dressed like native Americans and dumped all the tea from England destined for the colonials in Boston Harbor. It was the ultimate tea party, but different from the way the British were used to it. A bitter fight ensued between the British and American families. It was essentially a protest against Mother England and her domineering ways.

We also went to Harvard University to see the campus, as we were inclined to do whenever we were near a famous college. Harvard was as beautiful as one can imagine, with its Ivy League walls and ancient buildings with more history than Boston, even though Harvard was in Cambridge, just north of Boston. It would take four years to learn what every building is on this campus. Established in 1636, Harvard is one of the oldest in the country, and it has enrolled quite a few famous people, including eight presidents. Going to Harvard has to be the penultimate experience for an academic student. One can hear the brain power operating when one walks by the classrooms. It was just an incredible experience to walk through some of the academic halls and the campus. It was just magnificent and fun.

We got in the car and went to Lexington to see where the battle to start the Revolutionary War took place. It was where the first shot of the American Revolution was fired—the "shot heard round the world." It set off a confrontation with Britain that would last for seven years, from April 15, 1783, to September 3, 1783, when the Treaty of Paris was signed. The war had started because the colonists had enough of taxation, the Boston Massacre, the Boston Tea Party, and the Intolerable Acts. All of these combined with the willingness to fight for freedom from England. It was not a friendly encounter. It took 175 battles to decide this war, all of which were important to the survival of colonial America. We walked the bridge at Lexington, looked at the historical markers, and discovered that a war had taken place on American soil and would not be the last.

John Smith drew a coast map and called it New England in 1616. Then, the actual settlement of New England began. After the arrival of the Mayflower in 1620, ten years later, in 1630, John Winthrop established the Massachusetts Bay Colony with a thousand immigrants from England. There were Pilgrims and Puritans–Pilgrims wanted to separate from the Church of England (thus, Separatists), and Puritans wanted to stay in the church and "purify" it by ridding it of "pagan" idols. John Winthrop declares, "We shall build a city upon a hill; the eyes of all people are upon us." It was Beacon Hill in Boston that he spoke about. Boston was a town in Lincolnshire, England, where many Puritans and Pilgrims came. They established the first colony graveyard called King's Chapel Burying Ground. Most of the first generation of Puritan founders are buried there. We walked to the graveyard and looked back to the origins of our country.

CAPTAIN JOHN SMITH'S STATUE IN
WILLIAMSBURG, VIRGINIA

In Boston, the first church was built, the first public school was established, Harvard College in 1636, the first tavern, the first post office, and the first public library. By 1640, twenty thousand people lived in the greater Boston area. It was also here that any other religion was not welcomed. Quakers were banned from the area and threatened with the death penalty if they returned. While the Puritans may have come to America for religious freedom, it was just for their religious freedom and not anyone else's. This would take time to resolve, and other religious groups had to establish themselves elsewhere.

The Puritan-run General Court banned the celebration of Christmas because they objected to its "pagan" roots and its association with the Anglican Church. When Oliver Cromwell took over the rule of England from 1640 to 1660, he also banned Christmas in England. It would not be until the restoration of the monarchy and Charles II that trouble came to New England and, one hundred years later, the Revolutionary War. The Old South Meeting House, built in 1669, would be where the patriots met to plot the Boston Tea Party. Boston was the best place to start our history trip because the very foundation of our country was built upon a hill in that city, whether for good or bad. It was sometime in 1638 that enslaved people from Africa were seen in Boston. Thus, the second war on American soil would be fought over their freedom in 1860.

We learned a great deal during our stay in Boston: excellent food, wonderful people, and a fantastic town.

AUGUST 2, 2014

We left Boston for Provincetown, Massachusetts. On the way, we stopped at Plymouth Rock. We visited the Plimouth Patuxet Museums, where one could transport oneself to the early 17th century. When one enters the village, a sign says, "Welcome to the 17th Century." Indeed, we were transported to the time of the early settlement of the Plymouth Colony. This 17th-century English Village was a replica of the original settlement of the pilgrims on the Mayflower. The location of this village was not too far from the original settlement on Leyden Street. One can see the original houses' demarcations if one takes a short ride to look at them. Another two miles up the road was Plymouth Center, Massachusetts, where the town of Plymouth was established. The Mayflower Compact was considered the first document by which Americans were to live. It was the foundation of living for the people of the Mayflower.

What intrigued us the most was the Mayflower and a replica of it could be found in the museum. We learned that it arrived on the banks of Massachusetts when it had spent part of the winter off the coast of the tip of Cape Cod. We had to explore that site, so we drove the whole length of the peninsula and arrived in Provincetown. There, we found a museum with a replica of the Mayflower and the story of their stay off the waters of Cap Cod Point. It is called Long Point. Few people were there when we visited the museum, but the drive was worth the effort. We learned that only half of the Pilgrims survived the winter and that they had dropped anchor on November 21, 1620. They would go ashore at Plymouth Rock a month later. I was told by a professor at the University of California at Los Angeles that Dorthy Bradford, the wife of William Bradford, jumped off the <u>Mayflower</u> and drowned, killing herself. However, all the accounts I have read indicate that she fell accidentally and drowned in the freezing waters while her husband was away exploring a landing spot for the <u>Mayflower</u>. It was a tragic beginning for the Bradford family. Undaunted, William Bradford would rule Plymouth Plantation for thirty years as Governor.

We found Provincetown to be a lovely place but did not realize when we arrived that it was the location of the largest LGBTQ community in the country. We walked the town and found the entire place owned and operated by gay people. We just thought the whole thing to be ironic. The original arrival of the Puritans from England was now a gay community. Talk about America coming a long way! We stopped for lunch and thought the service, the food, and the atmosphere to be excellent and fun.

We went to see the Pilgrim Tower, which gave us views of the entire area from the top. The tower rises three hundred and fifty feet above sea level, so the view is impressive. It was just fantastic, and the beauty of the town could be enjoyed all the more from high above the landscape. It is a town full of artists and creative souls who painted, drew, and made pottery. It was a beautiful place. The Cape Cod Pilgrim Memorial Association built the tower to honor the Pilgrims' first landing in Provincetown. Teddy Roosevelt laid the first cornerstone, and William Howard Taft dedicated the finished tower in 1910.

**THE VIEW FROM THE PILGRIM MONUMENT
TOWER IN PROVINCETOWN, MASSACHUSETTS**

We had to leave, but we were better informed about the original landing of the pilgrims. We drove down the peninsula, found a hotel, and stayed the night near the coast to get to Nantucket Island.

AUGUST 3, 2014

Why go to Nantucket Island? Well, it was the world's whaling capital once in its history. The whole ambiance reminds me of the Herman Melville novel *Moby Dick*. We went not to see the whaling museum but just to get a sense of the place, given that it is so attractive to the rich. The island has some of the most beautiful beaches in the world, and they are mainly enjoyed in the summer. The island is known for its scenic beauty, natural beauty, beaches, and historic architecture. The houses are just magnificent and so pretty. The town was so quaint and lovely. It was a rich person's paradise, and many visited the island for the summer. We had a lovely lunch at Queequeg's because he was a central character in the novel *Moby Dick*. Eating seafood is the only thing to do on this island, and we indulged. Their Shrimp Scampi was divine, and so was the clam chowder. The Lobster Roll wasn't cheap but quite delicious.

NANTUCKET ISLAND, MASSACHUSETTS

We took a tour of the island and saw some of the more magnificent houses owned by millionaires and billionaires, of which sixty-five had residences. There were several golf courses on the island, and I would have loved to play any of them, but most of them were private, and it would take moving heaven and earth to get to play one of them. None of them are all that famous in the world of golf, but many of those who play them are. We were so pleased with our time on the Island that we wanted to see Martha's Vineyard, but getting to the island was just too tricky without waiting another day or two. We got back to the car in Hyannis Port and took the time to explore the town and try to see the John F. Kennedy compound.

The compound had three Kenney houses: Rose's, Jack's, and Ethel's. What a tragic family. Without going into the litany of tragedy that befell the Kennedy family, one wonders about the deaths of both John and Robert Kennedy. They fell before their time and before they could institute the changes in American society that they had envisioned; it makes me wonder what happened and why. Without knowing the answers to these questions, I believe their deaths signaled a change in our society, leadership, and sanctity as a country. We had lost our innocence and no longer lived in a world with safety for our leaders and citizens. Guns have destroyed our country, and they continue to destroy it daily. We live in dangerous times and under dangerous circumstances. When assassins killed the two Kennedys, we were an innocent country, but when they were felled, we lost that innocence and never regained it. The interpretation of the Second Amendment is one of the reasons why the decline of American Society is assured. We will have mass shootings and killings for a long, long time, and they will disrupt and disturb our society like never before. The cruel part is that so many mass murders happen in our schools, and our children are being slaughtered like lambs. What a pathetic society we live in—end of rant.

Hyannis Port was a great town to visit, but we had to go to the next destination: to visit a cousin of mine on Long Island, New York.

AUGUST 4, 2014

We had to drive to Westhampton Beach on Long Island, and it was an adventure. Gloria Labak Gewelke was my first cousin on my mother's side, and I wanted to share the information I had learned about our grandparents and visit her and her husband, Don. It was a fantastic day when we arrived after a long four-and-a-half-hour journey that was quite exciting. We arrived in time for drinks and dinner and had a wonderful time talking about family after not seeing one another for about fifty years. It is incredible how much cousins have in common, especially since we were the same age. We did not know each other well when we were younger, but shared some holiday time. Gloria was one of those knockout cousins that you couldn't take your eyes off of. She was as beautiful inside as she was on the outside when we shared our time with her and Don. We spent the night and then went to breakfast at a local restaurant the next day, where we shared more stories and more information about what we had done with our lives in the last fifty years. There was a lot of ground to cover.

COUSIN GLORIA LABAK GEWELKE AND NANCY DEVOGEL IN WEST HAMPTON, NEW YORK

Gloria's maiden name is Labak, and she is the third child of John and Helen Labak. Five children were in the family: Marlene, Suzy, Gloria, John, and Patty. Gloria is the first of the family that I got to visit, and I am hoping to see Patty on the way home to California. The family moved out to California in the 1950s, and then both sisters, Julie and Ann, followed shortly after. The fourth child, my Uncle Joe, stayed in Ohio.

One of the problems I found when traveling around the country to share the good news of the origins of my grandparents was discovering that families had split apart by geographic distance. The family unit has broken up by distancing itself from one another, and this has caused a great deal of problems with communication. Distances make for difficult communication because there are time differences that the family members have to deal with. This is just one factor in the demise of the family in our society. The separation of family members creates an out-of-sight, out-of-mind relationship. It is another nail in the coffin of the American family. It is dying by slow degrees. We enjoyed our time with the Gewelkes and moved to another part of the island to visit the home of Teddy Roosevelt.

AUGUST 5, 2014

We went to the house Teddy Roosevelt and his wife lived in their entire lives: Sagamore Hill National Historic Site, a home built in the 1880s. It reminded me of Twain's house partly because of the Victorian style. It was on a beautiful hill overlooking the area of trees and farmland. We were able to visit the house, and it was spectacular. There was so much to learn about the accomplishments of Teddy Roosevelt. There is no need to cover the accomplishments of this great president, but suffice it to say he did things in the public's best interest. Our national parks are there because Teddy felt they were necessary for public use in the future.

The area we visited was called Cove Neck, near Oyster Bay on the opposite side of Mill Neck. It reminded me of The Great Gatsby, but we found that the novel took place at Great Neck, where Gatsby's house was, and Port Washington, the East Egg, and Great Neck, the West Egg. Old money and new money lived on opposite sides, and driving through that area gave me the same view Nick Carraway, the book's narrator, had when he said, "So we beat on,

boats against the current, borne back ceaselessly into the past."
(Fitzgerald 280). Society is made up of what has happened in the
past. We discover why we are where we are when we discover our
history. That is what this trip is all about.

AUGUST 6, 2014

Our next stop this morning was at Princeton University. As I
had indicated, we loved visiting the great colleges around the eastern coast, and going to Princeton was just a total joy. It was by far
the prettiest campus of the Ivy League we had seen so far.

Although we have not seen all Ivy League schools, it would be
hard to argue that anything is as pretty and motivating as Princeton
University.

Princeton, New Jersey, was essential to the Revolutionary
War. After crossing the Delaware on December 25, 1776, Colonel
Washington embarked on a ten-day campaign to change the war's
course. Ultimately, the ten days ended at the Battle of Princeton
on January 3, 1977. George Washington had kept the hopes of the
Revolutionaires alive with these victories, and the colonists would
go on to win the war.

Before becoming Princeton University, the college was initially
called The College of New Jersey. It served as our nation's capital in
1783, where members of the Continental Congress met at the college. Three presidents lived in Princeton: James Madison, Woodrow
Wilson, and Grover Cleveland. The most celebrated majors to take
at the college are computer science, economics, political science,
and engineering. It is a great university to attend and one that was
so enjoyable to visit.

On our way down to Philly, we stopped at Washington's Crossing,
where George Washington crossed the Delaware and proceeded on
the campaign I just mentioned. The crossing is reenacted every year
in December to commemorate the moment. There is a stone marker

to indicate the departure point of Washington, and his crossing is made famous by the artist Emanuel Gottlieb Leutze, who was born forty years after the battle. He painted the famous picture in Dusseldorf, Germany. Leutze grew up in America but went to live in Germany as an adult. It is one of the best-known paintings in America, and it can be seen in the Metropolitan Museum of Art in New York. On one of our many visits to New York, we saw the painting, an unforgettable experience.

WASHINGTON CROSSING IN PENNSYLVANIA

When we got to Philadelphia, our first venture was to visit Independence Hall and learn about the Declaration of Independence and The Constitution, both written in that building. The Declaration of Independence was written, for the most part, by Thomas Jefferson. It declared our independence from Britain, the mother country where most people originally came to settle in America. The declaration is an argument laying out why we desire to be independent of Britain. When I taught American Literature, this writing was part of the colonial literature that students learned about. It was important for students to understand what it meant, why it was written, and why we celebrate July 4th every year. What I found interesting is people's reliance on the sanctity of the Founding Fathers. They were not perfect men. After all, despite declaring independence from Britain, we still held onto slavery. Although there were efforts to eradicate the practice, Colonial America needed more time to be ready to do so. Eventually it would cost us dearly, as we will see later on our historic tour since we plan to stop at Gettysburg.

INDEPENDENCE HALL IN PHILADELPHIA

We then moved to the other side of the building and heard about the development of the Constitution and the problematic struggle it was to agree on the language and laws. It was a long, arduous process to ratify the Constitution. It took several years and an enormous amount of debate. The significant debate was over states' power versus the central government's power. It is essentially the struggle between states' and federal government's rights. The Constitution replaced the Articles of Confederation, which gave the states too much power and failed to create an executive and judicial branch of government. The Constitution changed that, but initially, the Constitution did not have a Bill of Rights. Several months after the Constitution was adopted, the Bill of Rights was added as the first ten amendments. Since then, an additional seventeen amendments have been added to the Constitution.

The central failure of the Constitution was the addition of the 2nd Amendment—the right to bear arms. When the Constitution was drafted and the amendments added, guns were different than they are today. There is no need for military-style weapons in the hands of American citizens. They have caused more pain in our society than any other effects of rights in the Constitution. We cannot easily change the Constitution, even though most Americans do not think military-style weapons should be in the hands of American citizens. We will have many more mass murders; no one knows when and where they might happen. Today, our society suffers from those who argue that the Federal Government is too much in the way of one's freedoms and those who think it is the central government's role to control individual states' behavior.

From Independence Hall, we went to see the Liberty Bell, but the line was so long that we decided on lunch. The Reading Terminal market is a fantastic place for lunch because dozens of vendors want to serve the best lunch imaginable. We found a great Philadelphia Cheesesteak restaurant and chowed on that famous sandwich. It was just incredible. I will bet that the Framers of the Constitution did not have this kind of lunch in their day.

We jumped on a tour bus, circumnavigated the city, and learned about the city's significant buildings and historical markers. We saw the original house where Washington lived when he was elected president. It was not reconstructed, but an outline of the house allows visitors to walk around in it. Washington did not live in the white house because it was not completed then. Instead, he had a residence in Philadelphia and New York. John Adams, his successor, would be the first to live in the White House. Although Washington was president, plenty were seeking to hold the power of the presidency.

We also visited the Betsy Ross house to see where our flag was created. Although there was controversy as to whether she created the flag with the stars and stripes, it clearly shows how important she was to the patriotism of her country.

The American flag has become a weapon of patriotism today. One is not a patriot if one does not fly the flag on one's truck while driving. There is a kind of ownership of the flag and its meaning—one is a patriot if one flies the flag high and demonstrates one's fondness for it. One doesn't have to be a flag waver to be a patriot. I do not believe one has to honor a flag to honor one's country. One can be a patriot without an ostentatious display of flag waving. One can find a display of patriotism by supporting the men who fight for and die for their country.

AUGUST 7-9, 2014

The following day, we drove to Washington, D.C., and caught some hot weather. It slowed us down trying to see several of this unreal city's sites. We planned to stay an extra day. During our stay, we visited as many sites as possible. First, we say the three war memorials are the Korean War Memorial, the Vietnam Memorial, and the

World War II Memorial. Each of the memorials was distinctly different from one another, but the Vietnam Memorial was the most emotional. It was difficult to stand at the wall and look at all the names of those soldiers who lost their lives in that war. While the war caused civil unrest in America, I attended college from 1966 to 1970 during the worst part of that war. I continued with postgraduate work, used up my five years of postponement, and was drafted in the summer of 1971. When I got to the last station of the physical, a doctor declared me "4-F" or unfit for service because I had vitiligo on my body near my ribs. Vitiligo is a skin disorder that doesn't produce pigment in the skin and leaves it vulnerable to cancer. I could not be in the sun without a shirt, one for fear of contracting skin cancer. I went back to graduate school and finished my teaching credential.

While I admire the service of all the young men and women who served our country, I do not admire the decision-making of those who put us there. I heartily disagreed with our presence in Vietnam and was only one of two people in my government class in a room of 38 people to say no to it. The professor asked me why I was against the war; my argument was that war did not solve any problems. I was a pacifist and did not agree with war. During the Vietnam conflict, we lost 58,209 men and women. Each of their names was etched in stone on the memorial. It could make anyone cry. I did not agree with WW I but with WW II and none of the others that followed.

What is the United States of America? Are we a war-mongering nation that has to pick a fight or join a fight that is none of our business? What have we gained from any of the wars we have fought? Have we ensured freedom for Americans? Why do we have to go to war? Are we looking to exercise our new military equipment? I don't like the protracted war in Afghanistan, and I think we should get out. We spent eight years in Iraq, costing us too many lives and billions of dollars. What did we get out of that? Did Democracy come to Iraq? When I was a student in college, my English professor taught us a poem by Wilfred Own called "Dulce et Decorum Est" in Latin, meaning "It is sweet and becoming to die for one's country." Ironically, the deaths of all of our men and women in these wars cannot be described as sweet, although Owen was writing a poem of irony. When I was teaching in 2001, when the trade centers were bombed by our airplanes, many of my students wanted to join the army when they were out of school to get the enemy. I showed them the poem. It did not matter. They wanted justice for America.

The World War II Memorial taught us that 16 million people served in the armed forces during this war, and four hundred thousand soldiers died, saving the world from the tyranny of Hitler and Hedeki Tojo. When I visited Germany and Japan in the 1990s, I learned that the German people were not very proud of their history and spoke of other heroes of Germany but never mentioned Hitler. When my son and I were in Japan for three different golf tournaments, there was one time when we strayed into a bar in Japan and were told not to come in because the people there hated Americans, and this was fifty years after the war! The leadership brings us trouble in war, not the people themselves. We found that out through the Vietnam War. Perhaps the Japanese were bitter about using nuclear bombs on Hiroshima and Nagasaki. Robert Oppenheimer, the chief engineer of the bomb, said, "Now I become Death, the destroyer of worlds," a phrase he took from the *Bhagavad Gita*. He died at sixty-two in Princeton, New Jersey, on February 18, 1967. He did what he called his duty during the war and could not feel responsible for the decision to drop the bomb, even though he was instrumental in creating it. William Faulkner, a prominent novelist in American Literature, said in his Nobel Prize for Literature acceptance speech that there was only one question left for humanity: when will the next bombs be dropped?

WW II MEMORIAL IN WASHINGTON, D.C.

One of the worst statistics I learned about those three wars and those that followed was that 81,000 men are still missing. Imagine many men who never came home from war, even in a body bag. This is why I am opposed to war. Seven thousand five hundred of them are still unaccountable from the Korean War. Imagine that.

We then visited the Lincoln Memorial, the Capitol Building, and the Washington Monument. Although these visits took several days, we thoroughly enjoyed our visits to each of these memorials. The Lincoln Memorial has one of the best views of the mall and the Washington Monument. We also visited the steps of the Supreme Court and got memberships to the Library of Congress. Each visit took time, but we covered much of what we wanted to see. We did not get to see the White House Tour because entrance tickets had to be secured months in advance, and our timeline for this trip was uncertain. The Jefferson Memorial was ski[[ed] and the Smithsonian Museum because of time constraints. We were headed to Monticello after Mount Vernon anyway, so we would get a good education about Thomas Jefferson when we got there.

AUGUST 10-11, 2014

We left Washington D.C. and drove south to Mount Vernon, the home of the first President of the United States, George Washington. The home of George Washington is undoubtedly one of the best to see of all the presidents. It was a massive site that took a couple of days to explore. The house itself was one of the most beautiful homes of his day. In the house was a Blue Room, a Yellow Room, a Chintz Room, the Lafayette Room, and Washington's Bedchamber. It also included a front parlor, a little parlor, a study, a dining room, an old chamber, a new room, and a west front entrance. It also featured a sixteen-sided barn.

The massive complex of Washington's estate included a Smokehouse, Men's and Women's Slave Quarters, a Slave Cabin Yard, a Gardener's House, A Storehouse, Servant Quarters, a Salt House, and Overseer's Quarters, a Blacksmith Shop, a Spinning Room, a Distillery, and George Washington's Study. In this place, he dressed and did his business work. There was an Old Tomb and a New Tomb where the Washington's were buried. The estate also had a pioneer farm, a place for the animals, a slave memorial, and a gigantic gristmill.

Beyond all the buildings were two gardens, a fruit garden and a lower garden for vegetables. It was so large that it took a hundred enslaved people to attend to the work of both gardens and the grounds; George Washington lived from February 22, 1732, to December 14, 1799. He served as President of the country from 1789 to 1797, then went to retirement. He served as the "Father of Our Country" and was considered a brilliant man who made America a reality.

AUGUST 12, 2014

After sleeping near the home of George Washington and wondering if anyone was cutting down any cherry trees on his land, we took off for Monticello to see the plantation of Thomas Jefferson. Not only did Jefferson write The Declaration of Independence, but he also designed and redesigned his home in Monticello, Virginia. His home was the most organized of the homes we had seen of authors and historical figures. Jefferson was also the designer and founder of The University of Virginia, perhaps one of the most architecturally beautiful colleges in the country. He served as president from March 4, 1801 to March 4, 1809. Jefferson was a Democratic-Republican who opposed a strong central government and championed states' rights. The other party was the Federalists, who supported a strong central government.

The most significant accomplishment of his presidency was the Louisiana Purchase in 1803. America had doubled in size. His most significant controversy was fathering children with an enslaved person. He fathered six children with Sally Hemings. Their relationship still needs to be recognized by the Thomas Jefferson Foundation. Jefferson died in 1826 and freed Sally and her children. She did not live in the White House but bore three children while he was president.

Although his Monticello house was incredible, it was a work in progress. Jefferson felt that way throughout his tenure at Monticello and never stopped improving it. The house had many rooms, one of which was a library like no other. One can take a virtual tour of the house online. One unique fact about this house was the forty years it took to complete it.

**MONTICELLO HOME OF THOMAS JEFFERSON
IN CHARLOTTESVILLE, VIRGINIA**

The gardens of Monticello were terrific, and so much of it was still situated as Jefferson had envisioned it. There were acres and acres of gardens to maintain, and Jefferson had six hundred enslaved people to care for them. It was by far the most of any president. Even though he sought to establish a nation founded on the principles of freedom, there was just one problem: freedom was only for white people. Four hundred people worked at Monticello, and 200 worked at other properties he owned. They were owned by the man who advocated liberty. He did not hold the enslaved people for their benefit but for the benefit of his family. It did not matter if he was a "good" slaveholder because there is no such thing as a good slaveholder. I find those people who revere this country's "Founding Fathers" to be nothing but ignorant fools. Thomas Jefferson ordered physical punishment and left that work to overseers who performed physical violence whenever necessary.

One can be sure that Jefferson was indeed a "Founding Father." Even though he wrote that slavery was evil, he never freed most of the people he held in bondage. He was a racist and held the same views as many of his racist peers. No wonder the long-held notion of racism permeates the soul of American society if one of the significant "Founding Fathers" was a major contributor to it. Sadly, our governing forefathers were racists who believed that people of another color were enslavable. On our way out, we saw the gravesite of Thomas Jefferson, and the gates appeared to be closed. Good thing.

THOMAS JEFFERSON'S GARDENS AT MONTICELLO

AUGUST 13, 2014

We drove to Jamestown, Virginia, the first "successful" settlement of America in 1607. It was a fascinating experience. Jamestown is considered the original site of the Jamestown Colony and the birthplace of the United States. It was named after King James I of England. One hundred and four men arrived in January of 1607 on three ships: Susan Constant, Godspeed, and Discovery. All three ships could be viewed at the Jamestown Settlement, a museum with a recreated native American town not far from the Jamestown Colony. During that first winter, only 38 of the 104 men survived the winter. Over time, only 60 of 500 settlers could survive the winters. Today, the Jamestown Colony is an archeological site where discoveries are made about what happened to those settlers during those early years.

What is less well known is that it was also the site where slavery began in the colonies. Twenty or so Angolans that the Portuguese had kidnapped came to the colony of Virginia in August of 1619. Early America was a slave country almost from the beginning. This information antedated that which we learned in Boston.

Nearby was the Jamestown Settlement, a 17th-century Virginia history and culture museum. Near the site of the original colony, we discovered the story of America's beginnings through immersive films, gallery exhibits, and outdoor re-creations. We learned about the Virginia Indians who occupied the landscape for centuries, the arrival of English colonists to Jamestown in 1607, and the first documented arrival of West Central Africans in 1619, leading to cultural encounters and events that planted the seeds of a new nation.

JAMESTOWN SETTLEMENT IN WILLIAMSBURG, VIRGINIA

We managed to see the cultures of the Powhatan Indians, English, and West Central Africans who converged in 1600s Virginia—trace Jamestown's beginnings in England through the first century of Virginia colony life. Gallery exhibits incorporate new historical research and technology, rare artifacts, interactive displays, short films, and an experiential theater. We stepped back into the outdoor history areas where costumed historical interpreters described and demonstrated daily life in early Jamestown. Explore life-size re-creations of a fort and town or climb aboard a re-creation of one of the three ships that sailed from England to Virginia in 1607.

The most significant story out of Jamestown was the famous John Smith, the leader of the colony and the daughter of Chief Powhatan, Pocahontas. Although Disney would create a love story between the two, it never happened. When John Smith was captured, Smith wrote in his *General History of Virginia* that Pocahontas had risked her life to save his. Smith was captured and about to be executed when she placed her head on his and supposedly saved his life. This was more myth than reality. The Disney myth is that they had a love affair, but at the time of this incident, she was just eleven or twelve years old, and John Smith was thirty. Smith left the Jamestown colony because of a gunpowder wound and returned to England in 1609. Pocahontas married John Rolfe and had one child, Thomas. They went to England to live out their lives there. Powhatan had allowed her to marry Rolfe more to protect her from anything happening to her than full consent to marry Mr. Rolfe. By the way, the nickname Pocahontas means "naughty child" or "spoiled child." She went by Rebecca Rolfe in England.

Williamsburg was just fifteen minutes down the road, but we called it a day and would start fresh the next morning.

AUGUST 14, 15, 16, 2014

Williamsburg, Virginia, is Colonial history Disneyland. The entire place is a "reenactment" of 18th-century Colonial America. Williamsburg was the capital of the Virginia Colony from 1699 to 1780. There are five hundred restored initial buildings on the premises. The Rockefellers initially funded it to help recreate the period just before the American Revolution. When one walks through the town, character actors can direct one to anywhere one wants to go, and they often speak in an English accent of the 18th century. Sometimes, essential characters from that historic time will come out and address the gathered audience on an important subject. We were just amazed at how astute these actors and actresses were.

On one occasion, we listened to George Washington's speech and took pictures with him afterward. He maintained his "character" throughout our conversations with him. I believe he was a professor at a nearby university. I told him, "The lady you are taking a picture with is a descendent of your family." He looked astonished and then at Nancy and said, "Really?" He did not comment further as others were waiting to take a picture with him.

WILLIAMSBURG COLONIAL RECREATION IN WILLIAMSBURG, VIRGINIA

Historically, George brought his Continental Army to Williamsburg in 1781 for the siege of Yorktown, where the British surrendered and America was born. Williamsburg was the political, cultural, and educational center of what was then the most extensive, most populous influence of the American colonies. One can take a carriage ride and learn about this era. This is also the site of William and Mary's College, another beautiful college.

On one occasion, we saw a reading of <u>The Declaration of Independence.</u> It was dramatically presented, and the crowd was just wild with excitement. After the war, Williamsburg became the capital of Colonial New England. What struck us as unusual was the number of Blacks working the programs. It was indicated that as many as fifty percent of the population of Williamsburg were black. Systemic slavery was in full vogue in Colonial Williamsburg. The American War to resolve this was yet to come.

The taverns were fun and served great colonial food. We ate in three different ones; each was an authentic experience of food fare from that era. We loved it! There were hotels nearby, the Governor's Palace, a Market House, an Art Museum, and a merchant's store. We had a wonderful time here and were lucky with the weather since the place can be problematic in the summer with unbearable humidity.

We also enjoyed playing golf at The Green Course at Golden Horseshoe Golf Club and the Golden Horseshoe Course in Williamsburg. It was time to move on to another planned historic house, The Madison House, Montpelier, north of Richmond, Virginia.

AUGUST 17, 2014

It was a two-hour drive to James Madison's house, but we arrived just in time for the day's first tour. The plantation is called Montpellier, a famous resort town in France. Madison lived his entire seventy-six years of life at Montpelier. He is buried there at the family gravesite. Dolley was also interred there alongside James. James was the fourth president of the United States and the Father of the Constitution, derived from his writing called The Virginia Plan. During his administration, the British attacked America in the War of 1812. Several things happened that became legend.

Dolley Madison was said to have saved The Declaration of Independence during the siege on the White House, and she also saved a portrait of George Washington that hung at Montpellier for their entire stay there. Dolley was said to have hidden the Declaration in a suitcase and fled Virginia with it. During her stay at the White House, Dolley became famous for serving ice cream for dessert. She is said to have invented it, but other than that rumor, I know nothing about her creation story.

Montpellier is a National Historic Landmark given to the National Trust for Historic Preservation by the Dupont family, who owned the house until 1983. The house has since been restored to its original 22-room size. Montpellier is a 2650-acre property. Most of it is just beautiful land surrounding the house. At the height of his ownership, Madison had three hundred enslaved people. They did most of the work on the additions to the house.

JAMES MADISON HOME IN MONTPELIER, VIRGINIA

Although Madison fathered the Constitution, he was also a significant contributor to the amendments—of which there are twenty-seven. The first ten amendments are the Bill of Rights. While many people say that "the right to bear arms" is in the Constitution, it is not technically correct. The Bill of Rights was an amendment to the Constitution. The second right, the right to bear arms, has caused more consternation in this country than all other amendments combined. When I look at how our legislatures banned assault rifles at one time and then reversed that decision, it tells me that we might qualify as being one of the stupidest countries in the world. Serious problems continue to plague American society because of assault weapons, but we turn a blind eye to those problems to protect the right of everyone to bear arms. Why can't we all have tanks and bazookas and drones, then? How are these assault weapons any different than a hand grenade? I realize that many do not see it that way, but I do not think that the Founding Fathers of the Constitution intended for citizens to possess weapons of mass murder.

We left the Madison House and enjoyed the beautiful scenery as we drove north to Gettysburg, Pennsylvania, where guns, swords, knives, and canons slaughter many Americans.

AUGUST 18, 2014

Gettysburg was a three-hour drive from Montpellier but quite a beautiful one. Going to Gettysburg was the culmination of our historical trip around the Eastern part of the country. In a sense, if not in reality, the Civil War was a fight between two democracies whose visions of how to run the country were quite different. I have often said that our country is still in a civil war, but it is ideological. We have two major parties in our government, and both have differing views on many topics. Some groups have even armed themselves in the event of another civil war. We are a house divided, and the question is, will we be able to sustain this Democracy here in America? We are going the way of the Roman Civilization. We are not improving our society; instead, our society is in a death spiral.

Gettysburg was the bloodiest battle of the Civil War, although Antietam was quite bad for a one-day battle. Gettysburg was a three-day battle with 51,000 soldiers dying. They did not all die in battle but succumbed to their injuries. We were not medically equipped to save soldiers' lives on a battlefield then. It was Robert E. Lee's second attempt to invade the North and bring the war to an end, but the Union soldiers stood their ground, and the nation survived. Just think of it: the nation survived a bloody civil war, and many have still not gotten over that after over a hundred years of time passing. Despite being a terrible battle, the war continued for two more years after Gettysburg. All of those dead are interred in the National Cemetery.

On November 19th, 1863, Abraham Lincoln came to Gettysburg and addressed the nation. Lincoln says that our country's founders were dedicated to the proposition that all men are created equal. We fought the war to free the black man from slavery for many other reasons. Ever since the end of the Civil War, it has been a struggle for all men to have equal rights and opportunities in this country. I watched the battles on TV in Birmingham and the struggles for justice for black people in this country. Advocates for equal rights for all men were assassinated for wanting equality among our populace. John F. Kennedy, Robert F. Kennedy, and Martin Luther King all lost their lives, asking for the balance. There are so many opposed to this notion that they are willing to go to war again to fight for sovereignty and how they can live their lives. Although it appears that our country is free, it isn't: we are not free to say what we think or believe, for there are so many haters in this country who never want to see equality among men.

AUGUST 19, 2014

We drove home to Hellertown, Pennsylvania, returned to our routine, and went to the Thoreauvian garden to seek solace from our disturbing trip. We learned a great deal about the foundation of our country and the eventual Revolutionary War and Civil War. If we think we are living in troubled times, all we have to do is look backward and see the struggles that brought us forward to this time. F. Scott Fitzgerald was right: we are an accumulation of all our societies before us.

PART 6

HELLERTOWN, PENNSYLVANIA TO KEYSTONE, SOUTH DAKOTA

OCTOBER 7, 2014

More than a month has passed since Gettysburg. The garden is cleared for the most part. There are herbs and a few other things that are hearty enough for the coming frost. Once the frost comes, the garden is over. I have cleared the boxes for the most part, and I had Henry David Thoreau in mind when I was working. He said, "There is dignity in manual labor." I had to laugh at that quote. There is also a lot of back pain when one is done. Being sixty-six does not make working in the garden more accessible, but it was a good workout, and seeing what one has accomplished is always delightful. I also planted the Mums in the front yard--those yellow and purple ones are coming up from last year. I also had an area that was giving us a lot of trouble, so I just took everything down and planted grass. It is a lot less maintenance.

So, I am just about done for the summer here as the cold winds barreled down from the North last night. Fall has arrived in Hellertown, PA. The leaves changing colors is just one indication of the arrival of fall. Pumpkins are plentiful, the leaves are falling, the air is more relaxed, and the humidity has disappeared. It is a cool, crisp, sunny morning as I walk around the block with Nancy and the dogs. Here in Pennsylvania, one can measure one's life with the seasons. It is pretty and another reminder of the passage of time.

I will share the festivities with the reader on Sunday night just before I leave as my next piece of the travelog. Where did the summer go? I leave the reader with Emily Dickinson:

INDIAN SUMMER.

These are the days when birds come back,
A very few, a bird or two,
To take a backward look.
These are the days when skies put on
The old, old sophistries of June, –
A blue and gold mistake.
Oh, fraud that cannot cheat the bee,
Almost thy plausibility
Induces my belief,
Till ranks of seeds their witness bear,
And softly through the altered air
Hurries a timid leaf!
Oh, sacrament of summer days,
Oh, last communion in the haze,
Permit a child to join,
Thy sacred emblems to partake,
Thy consecrated bread to break,
Taste thine immortal wine!

It was an Indian summer and one of the best I have experienced in ten years in Pennsylvania. I will miss it, and Nancy, too.

OCTOBER 10, 2014

I will return to California starting Monday, but it will take me nearly a month. It will be the only time I will navigate the entire country, visiting cousins, checking off bucket list items, and stopping to see my family. I have a long trip, but winter will be a bit more challenging, so I will have to monitor the weather more. Time moves on. Seasons change. Life changes. It is good I take time to smell the roses. I am on the road on the 13th and returning to Canton, Ohio. On the way home, I will concentrate more on my mother's side of the family, although I will also see cousins from my dad's side. This Sunday is the 12th, Columbus Day, when Nancy Nicholson DeVogel was born.

OCTOBER 12, 2014

Nancy Nicholson DeVogel's birthday weekend is now over, and it just ended with the birthday party at a local restaurant called Braveheart. Friends and family gathered around and gave her a rousing Happy Birthday and many hugs and kisses. She enjoyed herself the entire weekend. Friday night, it was dinner at Cossi's and then the movie "Kill the Messenger." After the movie, I bought her a few books in the bookshop and then went to The Melt for drinks and music. We had a wonderful time. On Saturday, we went to another movie and saw "The Judge," another outstanding movie. Afterward, we went to dinner at Don Shula's. Today, we got up, went to church, and then to her birthday party at Braveheart restaurant in Hellertown. It used to be the old Hellertown Hotel, and the upstairs is a private room where we enjoyed drinks and a wonderful lunch.

All in all, Nancy had quite a birthday weekend. Here on Willow Avenue in Hellertown, some trees were planted fifty or more years ago and are starting to come down. They were the wrong trees for the neighborhood, with most lifting the sidewalks and making them "sidewalks." The trees have been falling or dying, and they are going the way of the dodo bird. They have served the neighborhood well. They gave the whole area that Ozzy and Harriet like of feel. But the area is old, and the trees and the husbands are the first to pass away. Nancy affectionately calls this "Widow Road," as many ladies are without husbands. My brother-in-law always tells his favorite joke about why men die first. He said, "Because they want to." And then Dan Watkins just laughs and laughs. I don't know. They determined that women have something better going on inside their cells. I just read it sometime back, and they think this cellular control thing allows them to live longer. So you see these older women in the front yard raking leaves and mowing grass. I have done Nancy's and the next-door neighbor's grass all summer. It is a good workout. Nancy becomes a winter widow because I refuse to shovel snow in the winter. I have a family I want to be with in the winter.

So, I will leave the reader with Sonnet 55 by Shakespeare about the passage of time and the fact that poetry is more resilient to time than the human body. Here it is:

Not marble, nor the gilded monuments
Of princes, shall outlive this powerful rhyme;
But you shall shine more bright in these contents
Than unswept stone, besmear'd with sluttish time.
When wasteful war shall statues overturn,
And broils root out the work of masonry,
Nor Mars his sword nor war's quick fire shall burn
The living record of your memory.
'Gainst death and all-oblivious enmity
Shall you pace forth; your praise shall still find room

Even in the eyes of all posterity
That wear this world out to the ending doom.
So, till the judgment that yourself arise,
You live in this, and dwell in lovers' eyes.

The poetry of William Shakespeare will outlive us all. He has given himself a kind of immortality. "So long as men can breathe or eyes can see, so long lives this, and this gives life to thee" are the last two lines of Sonnet 18. Poetry that lasts makes one immortal in a way. Emily still lives. Longfellow still Lives. Poe still lives. Anyone wants to live on, and the legacy of one's thoughts is one way to do it.

OCTOBER 13, 2014

I reluctantly left Hellertown, PA, and Nancy at 7:38 this morning and traveled across the state via the northern route 80 to Canton, Ohio. I am back where I was in late May only because this is the way to the Northern route across the USA. Two major highways to take are Interstate 80 and Interstate 90, both routes to the West. Eighty will take one straight to San Francisco, while 90 will take one to Seattle, WA.

Traveling along the interstate in the Northern part of PA, one is stunned by the beauty of the trees as they change colors almost before one's eyes. The experience reminded me of our trip to Vermont, where we walked ten miles daily between bed and breakfast places. We missed the red leaves in late October, but so much of it was just spectacular. I am sure there is much more of this coming in Michigan. I tried to take a picture of the trees out the car's window as I drove, but I am sure it did not do it justice. When I was driving North on 476 to get to 80, I saw a considerable mountain/hill in front of me, and it looked like a technic-colored wave rushing at me. As it turned out, it was just a mammoth hill I drove through via the Lehigh Valley Tunnel. It rained a bit along the way, but for the most part, the weather was good, just cloudy and cool.

One disturbing part of the drive was noticing all the deer hit by cars along the interstate. Driving at night along that highway will present drivers with some unexpected obstacles. These poor deer just find themselves in the wrong spot, looking to cross the highway to the other side for food or water. Seeing these lovely animals lying in contorted poses along the highway is so sad. It is man versus nature, with man winning most of the time, except for the damage the hit usually does to the cars. Sometimes, these encounters can be fatal for the animal and the driver. It happens more often than one cares to think about.

My travels had me only thinking of one person: my brother, Andy. He has some health issues, and I could only consider the challenges ahead. We all come into our family from a mixture of longevity and brevity. It is hard to say what genes one gets from the parents, but one can be sure that some take precedence over others. Anyway, I thought of the many times we shared conversations in the last ten years, and now I only pray for his return to health. I will not elaborate, but it was on my mind for many miles I drove today.

I arrived in Canton in the early afternoon, giving me time to do what I wanted. While I drove into the city, I found myself on familiar streets I had driven on when I was here in May. I returned to visit my grandparents' house on my mother's side in Southwest Canton. I found the house. I am almost sure it is the house of my grandparents. I had not even thought to look for the house the last time I was here because I was so focused on seeing all the cousins on my father's side.

JOHN AND MARY LABAK HOME IN CANTON, OHIO

Given that I had to go back through Canton on my way to Michigan, I decided to find that house, and I did. I remember the backyard and the side of the house, and I think it was the one my grandparents lived in after they gave the house that I lived in as a kid to my parents. It was a grocery store. My mother and father inherited my grandfather's grocery store. He ran the store from the early 1920s until approximately 1952. During that time, he also managed to acquire two taverns. One went to my mother's sister, and the other to the two boys in the family, my Uncle Joe and my Uncle John. As I have learned through talks with cousins, my grandfather was quite a guy. I admired his industry.

After seeing the house, which was empty and messy, I went to Calvary Cemetery, where my Labak grandparents are buried. I found them in the same general plot area as my father's parents on the opposite corner of the section. I stood there for a while contemplating the efforts of this man I had learned had come from Zilinia, Slovakia. I also learned that my grandmother had come from the same area of Slovakia, a place called Topolcany, but she and my grandfather never knew each other in Slovakia. Ancestry.com has nearly completed the research on my mother's parents, John and Mary Labak. Researching has taken a long time, but I know the truth. I learned that before WW I, twenty percent of all Slovakians left what was then the Austro-Hungarian Empire. After WW I, the country would become Czechoslovakia. In 1993, Slovakia became its own country, and the Czechs became The Czech Republic.

**JOHN AND MARY LABAK GRAVESITE
IN MASSILLON, OHIO**

So, I have learned that I am a second-generation, one hundred percent Slovakian. It is hardly a notable distinction, but it is at least the truth, and it is what I am ethnically. For the first time, I know this to be true and correct. It is incredible how many people don't know their ethnic origins. The PBS show "Finding Your Roots" is quite popular, and it has traced the origins of many famous people, some of whom discovered things they never would have known without that research. Knowing more than I do would be nice, but I have the foundation anyway.

Looking around at the setting for my grandparents made me happy to know they are in a wonderful place here on Earth. They rest peacefully in a beautiful setting. My grandfather Labak, my mother's father, gave what he could to his children. He was way ahead of his time. He wanted a better life for all of his children, a better life than he had. Isn't that what we want for all of our children, too?

OCTOBER 14, 2014

Today would have been my father's 100th birthday. He was born on October 14, 1914, in Canonsburg, PA. He was the sixth of eleven children. My dad was an outstanding athlete, playing professional baseball until he hurt his shoulder, then became a professional bowler, good enough to establish a four-game national scoring record. He spent much time in a bowling alley from the early 1950s until the early 70s before becoming a life insurance and real estate salesman. He would even have a career in his retirement as a singing senior who entertained 55 and older communities with his singing and joke-telling.

Dad came to Detroit in the 1950's and competed in PBA bowling tournaments. So, I am treading on the ground my father was on many years ago. I arrived in Michigan in the late morning, having left Canton, Ohio, for the last time. It was like a "Goodbye Columbus" day for me. Good-bye Canton. I have learned and seen as much as my time will allow me. Now, I am in Michigan. I think of Michigan when I traveled here in the 1990s for a golf tournament my son played up north near Traverse City. It was a beautiful area, and we had a wonderful time. So I have been here before.

Today, I explored what to do while waiting for a friend to arrive. I decided to see the Henry Ford Museum, and I want to see Ann Arbor, the magnificent University of Michigan college community. I will share that adventure with you tomorrow. I also spent time today exploring the history of my mother's father and mother through a conversation with a wonderful cousin, Tricia Labak

Golden. After yesterday's post, I learned I have a cousin who is just as motivated as me to learn about our past and who we are. She was a fountain of knowledge and wonderful to talk to about our grandfather and grandmother. We share a common interest in our heritage. Listening to Tricia Labak Golden motivated me to know more about the ancestral past. I know some people have little or no interest in it. Tricia and I are really into it.

Finally, I learned that Michigan is such a big apple state. The state produces 30 million bushels of apples yearly, which amounts to 700-900 million for the economy. They produce my favorite apple, the Honey Crisp apple. I learned that the Great Lakes surround this state. The state geographically looks like a dinosaur's head with its mouth open, and Canada is giving the dinosaur a sock in the jaw. I'm sorry to my Michigan friends if no one has ever made that observation. On the other hand, it is a beautiful state with tons of farmland and gorgeous trees everywhere. I am just getting started with Pure Michigan.

OCTOBER 15, 2014

What a day. First of all, it is my daughter Jennie's 35th birthday. She was born in 1979 and is technically a Generation X child, but bridges with the Millennials. She arrived at the end of one generation and the beginning of another. That makes her unique, and she is special. You see, she is just like me. The irony of life is that you think you should devote all the time to a child who is not like you, and you realize you should have devoted all the time to a child who is like you. But you realize it is what it is, and you do your best when in that situation. It all turned out well, as Jennie is a 2nd-grade teacher who has taught for ten or eleven years. I am so proud of her. When she was born, I called her Pumpkin Jen because she was born on October 15, 1979, and she was just my little Pumpkin. So I called her today and wished her a happy birthday and looked forward to seeing her in a couple of weeks. She is just an adorable person.

I woke up this morning and thought I needed to get going on my day of exploration in Michigan. So, I had two things on the agenda: get to the University of Michigan and the Henry Ford Museum in Dearborn, Michigan. So I got on the road, fought the traffic, and got to the University of Michigan at nine o'clock. It was amazing to be part of the campus for a half day and see the students attending class and trying to be part of the Michigan community. I took pictures of the campus and found it to be quite beautiful. I went to the football stadium and saw what I had seen on the television a thousand times: the Big House and The Big Blue. Oh, how I used to root against them when I was an Ohio State Buckeye and a fan of Ohio State Football. I used to have a couple of buddies in the golf group at Newport Beach Country Club who were just rabid Ohio State Football fans and who used to bet big-time on the games. We used to play golf in the early afternoon and get back just in time for the second half of the game to watch the Ohio State team win yet another one of their games.

MICHIGAN STADIUM IN ANN ARBOR, MICHIGAN

So, while there, I got around the campus with the help of students willing to point me in the right direction. I did not know where I was going, but the students' kindness allowed me to get where I wanted to go. I wanted to see the main campus, and I wanted to see the famous football stadium of the University of Michigan. I could not go inside Michigan Stadium, but I got close. The campus is just beautiful and an incredible place to go to school.

I was walking back to my car to my next destination and decided to get some lunch. I entered a Mediterranean fast food place and stood behind a student buying a wrap sandwich. He did not have enough money to buy what he wanted, so I offered him the two dollars that he was short. He kindly thanked me and was eternally grateful for the small kindness of my offer despite the fact we had no conversation. I remembered what it was like being a student in college and how little money I had. I saw this guy trying to get lunch, and the vendor wanted almost eleven dollars. I could not imagine being a student today in college with the amount of money it costs to get through school. Wow. The debt today that students have for loans to get a college education is nearly one trillion dollars. Can you imagine that? The Millennial Generation has been saddled with that kind of debt. We have it all wrong in this country about educating our children. The state should provide them with an education and leave their lives free from living under so much debt. My son's wife went to the University of Dublin and paid nothing to attend. Europe is more intelligent than we are regarding providing an education for their children.

The University of Michigan is just a wonderful place to go to college, and I like the community at Ann Arbor. The kids were great and so friendly and respectful to me. I was highly encouraged by their behavior and the youth of the Millennial Generation. The campus was enormous, and I got tired walking around it, but it was a good exercise. I could not believe the number of places to eat around the campus. The sororities and the fraternities could have been better taken care of. Their houses were dilapidated, and their care could have been better. I have seen beautiful houses on college campuses. The buildings were old and new, making them unique. I left the college feeling good and had accomplished my goal of visiting one of the finer college learning centers in the country. It was also fun to stand near the Big Blue stadium.

I then went to the Henry Ford Museum and walked there for nearly three hours. I cannot believe I saw just twenty percent of what Henry Ford had accumulated in his lifetime. Look at some of the incredible stuff he thought was essential to keep in perpetuity. He has millions and millions of artifacts that were from another time and place in life. After a while, I thought I could not understand why he took so much time accumulating things. These things are meaningless. Look at the sterling silver place settings, and you wonder what this has to do with it. Can you enjoy it now, Henry? Could you take it with you? Did killing yourself for money make you happy? Were you able to take your money with you? How about one of your cars? Did you drive it to heaven? It reminds me of the play "You Can't Take It With You" by George S. Kaufman and Moss Hart. Henry has none with him now, so why bother accumulating all of it? I still think the Ford Foundation is cheesy for charging the five bucks for parking when it does not say there is a fee until you enter the museum. Very cheesy. Very greedy. Corporations will monetize anything.

I ended the day by picking up my long-time friend from Newport Beach Country Club, who is a native of Michigan and went to school here before getting a degree and a law degree from the University of Colorado. So I picked him up at the Detroit Metro Airport and met his friend from Oakland Hills Country Club. We met him at a restaurant in Bloomington, and we had a wonderful time getting drunk and telling stories about the golf courses we have played and the pros we have had contact with---it was typical male stuff. We returned to the hotel and talked about life and what we were doing with it. It was difficult as Ed, one of my best friends, is battling cancer, so life is complicated.

OCTOBER 16, 2014

Oakland Hills Country Club is in Bloomington Hills, Michigan. It has been the host to many major golf tournaments. It is one of Donald Ross' finest designs, and I have the privilege of playing it today. It was incredible, and it was pretty tricky. The rating from the back is 76.9, and it is a par 72. What that means is that this course is so challenging from the back that Par is 77. That's right: 77. So if one shoots a 77 from the back, that is as good as par, and if one shoots a 72, then that is as good a five-under-par. The slope rating is 145, which is a challenging golf course. And it played it. I cannot believe how fantastic and how challenging the golf course was. I parred the first hole like it was nothing.

I played with my buddy, Ed Malpass, and he knew the member who invited us to play the course. The golf course was every bit as challenging as it appeared to be. The first few holes were less challenging than I had expected. Ed spoke about the course as if it were the lesser of the two courses, and I said, "How can that be? This course is challenging. Those who don't play golf can play from different tee boxes, meaning different distances. We played from the white tees, and it played 6560 yards but played longer because the grass did not allow any roll of the golf ball much, the air was dense as if it were going to rain, and the wind was blowing enough to make a difference in club selection. We went around in just over three hours, and it was a wonderful experience. Tomorrow we play the other course, the North course, which is supposed to be a lot easier.

The championship course has played host to several major tournaments. Jack Nicklaus and Gary Player were winners here. The entire place is just a significant memory of major golf championships.

The United States Amateur is there in the summer of 2015 again. What a complicated and lovely place.

OAKLAND HILLS COUNTRY CLUB IN BLOOMFIELD TOWNSHIP, MICHIGAN

OCTOBER 17, 2014

Today was another golf day at Oakland Hills CC and another fun day. The weather was a bit colder and windier, but the day was warm enough not to affect the golf. Donald Ross designed two spectacular golf courses; the North Course was much kinder. I birdied the first hole and had a few more opportunities to make more, but putting is one of the golf course's defense mechanisms. Those elevated greens are another defense that eventually laid into my score, but I scored about the same as yesterday. We played from 6550 yards. I also have many pictures of this magnificent golf course, the North course, a Par 70 that was not quite as tough as the South course but just as beautiful and fun. A special thank you to Tom Howell, the member at Oakland Hills that allowed us to have two days of spectacular golf and to allow us to enjoy lunch on the grill. Ed and I were just stunned when we were looking at Al Kaline, the famous Detroit Tiger who carried the team for several years in his career. Thanks, Tom Howell, for a beautiful time at Oakland Hills Country Club.

OCTOBER 18, 2014

I left Troy, Michigan, early in the morning to drive to Woodstock, Illinois. The reader may remember I met guys from Woodstock, Illinois, in an Irish Bar in Augusta, Georgia. They then invited me to play Augusta Country Club with them, and I did so. It was one of the finest experiences of my life. We had such a good time. They invited me to Woodstock, Illinois, on my way home. So I drove into town for two reasons: one was to play golf with these guys at their country club, Bull Valley Country Club, and the other was to see Woodstock, where they filmed the movie *Groundhog Day*.

BULL VALLEY COUNTRY CLUB IN WOODSTOCK, ILLINOIS

I drove to the golf course and met Mark Ritchie, and we chatted and watched the Iowa versus Maryland game. He got dressed, and we went to town to have lunch. He and I had a lot of fun conversing about many different things. After lunch, we returned to the golf course, got the clubs out, and went golfing. The course was beautiful. I did not play well because my back was acting up, but it was a delightful afternoon anyway. Once we finished golf, Mark took me to the hotel to check in, and then we went to town to take pictures of it.

I loved the movie Groundhog Day because it is a sophisticated statement about life. One can go through life grumbling and seeing the negative side, or one can go through life looking at the positive side. The glass is either half full, or it is half empty. Which is it? I met two guys on this trip who are like the "good" Phil Connors, the movie's protagonist. Tom Howell and Mark Ritchie. Both of them are upbeat, cheerful, and adorable fellows. They are the better side of Phil Connors. Perhaps the attitude one carries has a lot more significance in it than most people think. I met many people along the way, and it is always revealing how people come across to me as they serve me during my travels. Some people are just downright downers, and others are the complete opposite.

WOODSTOCK SQAURE IN WOODSTOCK, ILLINOIS

Mark then invited me to dinner at the club. It was a lovely place to eat and a very friendly club. The dinner was fabulous, and what made it special was that he just dragged out a couple of bottles of wine from his locker, and we drank some perfect Cabernet. Then I found out how expensive the bottles of wine were, and I flipped. They were 150-dollar bottles of wine. I knew there was a reason why they tasted so good. It did not end there. We met a friend of Mark's at the club, and he invited us to come over and watch the Notre Dame and Florida State game. We drank more and more wine, and by the end, I was glad that Mark was smart enough to take me from the hotel to the country club and then back to the hotel. What a guy! He knew he would get me smashed, so he carefully drank himself, and I got bombed!

Well, because it was such good wine, I had no morning aftereffects, and I popped out of bed, into the shower, got dressed, and went down the road to Hannibal, Missouri.

OCTOBER 19, 2014

I left Woodstock, Illinois, around 7:30 in the morning and drove to Hannibal, Missouri. I wanted to go to Hannibal to see where my hero, Mark Twain, was born and raised. It has always been a desire of mine to see Hannibal, the town on the Mississippi that gave us Mark Twain and, consequently, *Tom Sawyer* and *Huckleberry Finn,* two American classics. The town was every bit as wonderful as I thought it would be. It is so lovely and well-kept. They had a market fair in the middle of Main Street, so the pictures don't do the town justice, but I had to deal with what was. What I enjoyed most was seeing the boyhood home of Mark Twain, Becky Thatcher, Huck Finn, and Tom Sawyer. It was all good, and I enjoyed it a great deal. I saw Mark Twain as a bigger-than-life figure who contributed a wondrous amount of humor in his works and many more life lessons than one can imagine. The entire town is devoted to making money off the figure of Mark Twain. Twain would probably love knowing that.

MARK TWAIN TOWN OF HANNIBAL, MISSOURI

Mark Twain had great insights into the human condition and reached for some of these observations at the expense of all bystanders. He is an exploiter, but he includes himself in these beautiful musings. "Go to heaven for the climate and hell for the company," he quipped. Twain was a knowledgeable person who was well-read and well-traveled. He used to say there is nothing more than travel to reduce one's prejudices.

Mark Twain did not stay in Hannibal, Missouri, but he spent enough time there to get to know the people he would write about later in life. He was born in 1835, and by 1865, he was published, but it would not be until 1874 that *Tom Sawyer* would come out, and in 1885, that *Huckleberry Finn* would be published. It would take him nearly eight years to finish *Huckleberry Finn*. A narrative problem developed when writing the book, and he did not know how to solve it. Twain had the problem of Huck and Jim running South when Jim was not a free man. He had to invent a reason for the two doing that, so he introduced the Duke and the Dauphin to join Huck and Jim. Twain did not think that slavery was right, but I suppose he had to be careful with what he said, living in the South and a slave country. The novel *Huckleberry Finn* does not address the issue of slavery directly, but Twain implies that African Americans should have their freedom, and he gives that freedom to Jim at the end of the novel. The novel flirts with tragedy but is a comedy. It is a comedy because it has a happy ending. Tom survives being shot in the leg, the passing of the Widow Douglas frees Jim, and Huck "lights out for the territory ahead." That's what Twain did when the Civil War broke out. He headed West to become a reporter for the Sacramento Bee and take on additional adventures. But if there is any statement Twain makes about slavery, it is through his actions.

I visited his boyhood home (which has been reconstructed) and several places associated with him in the town. It took about three hours to go through all the stuff you get to see for a mere nine dollars. It was interesting. This town loves its fame, and they are all over the Becky Thatcher (Tom Sawyer's girlfriend) and Tom Sawyer look alike contest. They were having a street fair, so getting the right photos of the main street was hard.

I have finished the trifecta now: the boyhood home of Mark Twain, the home he loved and lived in Hartford, Connecticut, and his final resting place in Elmira, New York. If I had my life to live over again, I would have been a Mark Twain scholar, as I have already indicated. I would have loved every minute of it, learning more and more about the guy I regard as just as insightful into the human condition as William Shakespeare. I'd say I have put him in pretty good company.

OCTOBER 20, 2014

I took off from Hannibal, Missouri, early in the morning and went to Sioux City, Nebraska. Along the way, I experienced the sunrise and sunset in the middle of the country. The sunrise was behind me when I was driving west from Hannibal. It was a giant red ball, and it was impossible to look in the mirror and look at that thing. It was imposing. It was a different sun than I had ever seen, and it reminded me of the sun coming up in Japan. However, the sun is enormous in Japan and pops out of the ocean. It is amazing. In the middle of our country, the sun is low and spread like a star, with pointed rays emanating long distances from its center. When the sunset came, it was a giant yellow ball with large rays doing the same thing as it set into the horizon. It is impressive. I tried to take a picture of it, but I am still determining how good they will be. I am sure it will be better than what I saw.

Along the way, I was traveling at 65 miles per hour on US 36, an excellent road, when I looked in the mirror and saw a four-by-four race right at me at a high rate of speed, and I just froze. He swerved around me to the right and then back into my lane, and my heart stopped. Just as he raced by me, a highway patrol was coming the other way, but a big medium separated the highway. The four-by-four tried to slow down, and he did temporarily. Then he just disappeared out of sight. I drove along, and no one was near me, either in front or behind me. I was going just 65. I am in no hurry, so I do drive the speed limit. Suddenly, I looked in my mirror, and another car came at 100 mph. I immediately moved over. It was the highway patrol! I drove about another two miles, and sure enough, he pulled over the guy who raced by me. Let me say this about the highways of America. They are very closely guarded! In Ohio and Michigan, I have never seen so many highway patrols. One day in Michigan, I saw twelve pulled-over cars.

As I drove around the country, another memory stuck with me. I noticed some of the bridges or portions of the highway named after an officer who had lost his life in the line of duty. I have seen several of these memorials as I have driven across the country. I both respect and fear the highway patrol. They have a tough job guarding the highways of America and making them safer for those of us who travel them. However, I do not care for the one thing they do that annoys me. They sit at the bottom of the downhill highway and wait for those who let their speed get out of control going downhill. I watch my speed when I go downhill and take my foot off the gas. So far, I have been lucky not to get caught speeding, as I have inadvertently gone too fast. I have gone too fast a few times, but I need more to make a mistake. Though their job is tough, I do not envy what they do. Those looking to break speed limits have a chip on the shoulder, just for starters.

Another thing I see around the country is football stadiums at high schools everywhere. We are a football country. That is not an outstanding observation, but the naiveté that people allow their kids to play the game makes the focus so huge. I did not want my kid to play the game. I think it is dangerous, leading to long-term issues with the body for one's life. I know everyone can decide about this game, but to me, it is more trouble than it is worth. Too many football players have suffered brain injuries that debilitate them for life. I am glad that action has been taken to make playing more safe.

This country is so much like a giant farm. I cannot believe the amount of farmland that we have. We are indeed the breadbasket of the world. I have seen miles and miles of wheat and corn. We have a great deal of farmland. I am just disturbed by who is buying it. A foreign country should not be able to own our farmland. It is not American, making me wonder why a foreign country wants to grow on our soil.

OCTOBER 21, 2014

I left Sioux City, Nebraska, early in the morning, and it was only a short time before I was in South Dakota on my way to Mount Rushmore. I would travel north on Interstate 29 until I got to

Interstate 90, and then I went west. Driving on Interstate 90 is quite an experience. It is long, straight, and wide open to the fields of South Dakota. If I saw one black steer, I saw a thousand of them. It is Black Angus country. There were hundreds and hundreds of them roaming the hills and flat lands of South Dakota—quite a sight. Americans love their meat.

Another troubling sight was the billboards that lined the highway to Rapid City. It is part of what makes America ugly. Billboards. They are unsightly, and they are abundant. They mar the beauty of the landscape and indicate our need to advertise at the expense of the beauty of our environment. You would not see this in any country in Europe. It just makes common sense not to litter the environment with billboards. I may have hit on this subject before, but it deserves another comment. There has to be a better way for business owners to get people to see and stop at the door of their business to spend money. There is a better alternative than dotting the roadside with such hideous-looking signs. It is enough said.

Interstate 90 is the first highway that I have seen with a 75 MPH maximum speed, and many drivers who drive on it daily take the liberty of going 85 to 90. While I was driving 70, I was just standing still. The most remarkable thing is that only one highway patrol was on duty during the 350-mile drive. I still didn't take any chances and did not see one person pulled over. The Interstate is impressive.

South Dakota is a windy place. There is a lot of activity to build wind farms up there. They (whoever they were) were taking giant windmills to install as quickly as one can get to it. The trucks haul these giant windmills, going down the freeway one after the other. We are building windmills like crazy. Oh, and it is a bit windy in South Dakota. I already said that. I watched these guys working on the freeway as I drove across the state, and the wind blew them all day. It was like I was driving sideways.

I saw a sign selling houses in South Dakota if you want to move there. They were 43 dollars a square foot. Wow! It is dirt cheap for a residence, but I am sure the heating bill is relatively high, and the food is not any cheaper than anywhere else in the country.

I got gas at one South Dakota station and paid 2.86 a gallon. I could not believe how low that was! The temperature today was 75 degrees, and last year, a guy told me there was 28 inches of shoveling snow on October 3rd. My timing is good. Timing is everything in life.

I passed the house of Laura Ingalls Wilder and George McGovern. I had no time to stop, so I just drove on. It is a long way across this country, and I have to keep a schedule of being in Seattle by this weekend. I can't wait to see my daughter, Jennie, and her husband, Matt. And my sweet granddaughter, Kennedy.

When one drives along the highway for as many miles as I do, it is incredible to think that someone had to do the work to put all those telephone poles and electrical wires out on those hills. How did they do that? In some of the most desolate areas of the country, there they were: the giant high electrical towers and the telephone wires. It is just difficult to think how they did it. It was challenging work by dedicated men. America has hard workers.

Finally, my day ended with my arrival at Mount Rushmore, and I spent 2 to 3 hours there looking at all the films about how this wonder was built. There is a long story behind the monument's building, but it took seventeen years to get all the presidents carved into the mountain. There were four great ones: Washington, Jefferson, Teddy Roosevelt, and Abe Lincoln. Each has contributed to the advancement of this great republic. We think of them as being respected in their times, but Lincoln was assassinated, and Jefferson had children by his slave, Sally Hemings. Washington and Jefferson had myriads of enslaved people. Teddy Roosevelt was a great choice. Lincoln was a great choice. There is a bit of tarnish on them, given that the development of the early republic did not decide the solution to the issue of slavery. The declaration that all men are created equal did not apply to all souls. It would take a significant civil war before all that was decided. That has not ended discrimination. America still needs to be ready for a change. It will take a lot longer than my lifetime. A lot longer.

MOUNT RUSHMORE, KEYSTONE, SOUTH DAKOTA

PART 7

KEYSTONE, SOUTH DAKOTA TO YOUNTVILLE, CALIFORNIA

OCTOBER 22, 2014

I left Keystone, South Dakota, early in the morning to go to Yellowstone National Park. I knew it would be a long drive, and it was! It was only a short time before I was in Wyoming and then Montana. Both of those states are as pretty as they get. I loved Wyoming, and I could not get enough of Montana. The pure natural beauty of those two states is just something to behold. So far, I have been quite fortunate with the weather. Many spots along the way indicated the freeway was closed if the lights were flashing. Last year, this time, it was terrible already. I would not have been able to do what I am doing, traveling the high road (Interstate 90) versus the low road (Interstate 80). I am lucky so far.

The highway (Interstate 90) is a spectacular road that allows people to travel to the northern states more quickly. There is just a big problem in the winter, but who wants to be traveling then? The season is over at Mount Rushmore and Yellowstone, with many closings. People are tired from the summer, and the season is dwindling with fewer and fewer people. The only people showing up here are the ones who do not know any better, as the weather can be a factor if it turns sour. The warm weather will still be here for the rest of the week, so that I can get to the West Coast before inclement weather.

No actual observations are to be made today. I only saw one highway patrol, and the highway in Wyoming allowed us to go 80 miles per hour. I have never driven at a constant 80, but it helped. I drove for 8 hours today and finally got to Yellowstone, only to realize that it is a 51-mile drive to Old Faithful, so I turned around and decided to see it the next day.

OCTOBER 23, 2014

I woke early to go to Yellowstone National Park to see Old Faithful go off. I took pictures along the way and found that the park has about a million photo opportunities. It is a photographic dream natural wonderland, as I know my friend, Don Lyons, would attest. He is an accomplished photographer who was there recently, no doubt taking pictures of some of the things I was taking photos of. I have seen much of his work on Facebook and admire his passion for that hobby. The photos are of John Muir quality.

The drive from the north entrance was a 51-mile hour and a half jaunt that I found problematic when I got within 15 miles of it. The roads were all torn up. However, given that the park is 6500 feet in the air, I was pleased that I could even get to Old Faithful. The weather has just been spectacular, and I could not have been happier seeing this geologic wonder at such a late time in the season.

There were few people there when I got there. There were just two people, and they seemed to want to stay to themselves. After stalking around the area, looking at all the seating and facilities built for the geologic wonder, I stood there with my camera, waiting to see if anything would happen. I then engaged in a conversation with the two people there who were from Normandy, France. The husband could have spoken more English, but the wife was quite good at it. We enjoyed chatting about touring the country and going to different places. I said I had toured France before I toured my own country!

Before long, several more people arrived, and one older lady indicated that the visitor center said it was about to go off in 3 minutes! I asked her how they know when it will go off. She said they measure the geysers' times and heights to determine when the next one will go off. They happen about every 40 minutes. I did not have to wait very long, and off it went! It was spectacular, as one will see from the myriad of photos I took of the geologic phenomenon. The older lady from Helena, Montana, indicated that one of the geysers goes way higher but only goes off every 6 hours, and one of the geysers happens to go off every 20 years!

OLD FAITHFUL GEYSER, YELLOWSTONE
NATIONAL PARK, WYOMING

The whole park is full of geysers. Today, it was also filled with old geezers. I wondered how this came about, but I had learned from a Nova program that this area is a giant volcano. It is one of the volcanoes that could go off in a realistic amount of time since the last time it went off was 320,000 years ago. It is due. Ironically,

Old Faithful may not be so faithful if the whole volcano goes off to end the planet as we know it. Then it would be Old Unfaithful.

Geologic wonders like this make me realize how tenuous life here on earth is. We get hit with an asteroid, and that is it. We have one of the super volcanoes go off, and that is it. We have a significant tectonic plate move, and that is it. An uncontrollable virus comes along, and that is it. Ah, there are so many ways to die. What will happen, though, in the meantime is the opportunity to see as much of this good old earth as I can in my short time left. This was just another bucket list item for me, and it was so worth the effort. Yellowstone National Park is so big that it would take a week or so to explore it fully. I saw the topography and the seething earth. I hope it holds out for centuries to come.

I then drove to Spokane, Washington, and the drive through Montana and Idaho was unreal. I could not believe the gas prices as I drove through Montana. It was mainly in the low 3s and even lower than three at some stations. This is where it should be all the time. Even the Saudis think that oil should be at 82 dollars a barrel. However, when those Wall Street jerks get a hold of it in their "futures" trading, they increase prices. I am sick of Wall Street and what they do to our stocks and what they do to oil. Oil should not be traded on the stock market!

I saw a sign that said, "Jesus is the Lord of this Valley." That sounds like not being able to have religious freedom in this valley, but this is not what everyone believes in Montana. Jesus would not have wanted anyone to exercise religious intolerance. He was an open-minded individual. He would have welcomed all religions.

I saw a sign that said, "hand-rolled biscuits" at Cracker Barrel, a popular Southern restaurant. The problem with the sign was that the dough had a rolling pin running over it. Go figure.

OCTOBER 24, 2014

I drove from Spokane, Washington, to Seattle, Washington, a mere four-and-a-half-hour drive at a comfortable, leisurely pace. It was Friday, and I only had a little traffic. Even better, it was not raining. The east side of Washington was colorless, flat, and unusual. It was a plateau, and I do not know what that is supposed to mean in geologic terms, but it was not pretty. Given all the rain in Washington, there is nothing but green everywhere. That is just not so.

What I did see was quite unusual is that they grow a great deal of hay in the middle of the state. Stacks and stacks and stacks of hay, with hay trucks everywhere hauling it to some destination I need to be aware of. One would see these substantial dome-like structures covering the hay stacks, and it seemed like an endless supply. I never thought I would think of Washington as a hay country.

I arrived at my daughter's house around 2:30 in the afternoon and went to the store to get a few things for the weekend. I then had some lunch at a local restaurant and waited for my daughter to come home from school. My daughter, Jennie, is a second-grade teacher at Endeavor Elementary in Issaquah, Washington. She and her husband, Matt, live in Seattle in a section of Seattle called Queen Anne. They fortunately have their own house. When I arrived, I met the new member of their family: Berkeley Bear Waterman, a combination of Husky and yellow Labrador. She is just incredible. The first order of business was to take Berkeley on a walk.

We took a long walk, and Jennie showed me their neighborhood and the local elementary school. The local elementary school is just beautiful. The whole area is lovely, and people are friendly. We enjoyed the afternoon together, talking until Matt came home, and then we watched the Cal game as they took on Oregon. Cal got squashed, but we enjoyed the chicken soup that Jennie had prepared for dinner. It was a fantastic start to the weekend.

OCTOBER 25, 2014

Jennie and I took off for a couple of appointments in the morning, visited her school, and did some work. That is the kind of dedicated teacher she is. After a quick trip to one appointment, we visited her school in Issaquah, Washington. It is about a 25-minute drive from Seattle going east on Interstate 90. It is in the suburbs of Seattle. The school is relatively new and only about fourteen years old. We went to her classroom. I helped her file some things there, and we talked about education.

I cannot tell you how amazing it is to see Jennie's dedication and understanding of educating second graders. The work it takes to organize these lessons is just incredible. I learned that education at that level focuses on developing literacy and increasing math skills. This is not your father's or our curriculum when we were second graders. The sophistication is incredible. We spent much time discussing some of the problems associated with teaching today. Just as one would assume, the difficulties of teaching are tied to the problems with the home. Only fourteen of twenty-two of her students had finished the last homework assignment. Despite making the homework quite simple and uninvolved, too many families are not taking enough interest or securing the duties of their children when they come home at night to do some tasks related to the day's lessons. It was an experience I had for many years. Students began to dictate the pace of the curriculum in the classroom by refusing to do homework. Somehow, they felt the time was "their time," and no teacher would impose on them what anyone could do with "their time."

This is a subject with which I am familiar, and I know what it was like to make an assignment for students only to get one-third of them to come back the next day with the lesson prepared. What has happened to the duty of doing homework? Why do parents think that it is outside the educational process and that teachers need the support of parents to ensure that homework is done promptly? It is something that I fought the students during the entirety of my career, and one for which there was never a solution.

I learned that my daughter, Jennie, is an outstanding teacher who is incredibly well-organized and totally on top of what she does in the classroom. Her website for parents is just unreal, with every detail about their child's education covered, so other teachers even copied it because they wanted it to look as good as Jennie had done. I am incredibly proud of Jennie and loved talking about education with her in the classroom for over two hours. What a lucky bunch of kids.

**MY DAUGHTER JENNIE AND BERKELEY
BEAR IN SEATTLE, WASHINGTON**

The rest of the day was just an endless stream of sports on TV as it rained hard all day. We watched the Sounders play LA and win decisively, and then one football game after the other with sandwiches, pizza, beer, and wine. It was a great party day.

OCTOBER 26, 2014

I spent the day on Sunday with Matt and Jennie Waterman and their beloved dog, Berkeley Bear Waterman. When I was leaving for the store, Berkeley came to the window to see me off, and I took a picture of her. We had a wonderful day walking the dog, watching the Seattle football game, and enjoying some libations and great food. What I enjoyed most were my conversations with Jennie and Matt. They are part of the Millennial Generation. They were such good conversationalists; seeing how informed they were was amazing. I was flabbergasted by both of their insights into the world we live in. I was so heartened by their understanding of the world and the living situation in this time, this place, and this country. I was just so impressed.

I loved my time with my daughter and her wonderful husband, Matt. He is an excellent-looking fellow, and how well he has done with his life. I am just as proud of him as my daughter Jennie. He has done beautiful things with his life, and I am very heartened by this Millennial Generation. I wish for good things to happen for them. They are just wonderful people. I had so much fun with them.

I got a call from a cousin of mine whom I had met in Canton, Ohio. His name is Jerry Sinay. He has some children near Seattle and was there on a visit. He asked me to come by for a celebration to meet some of his children and party. Moreover, he wanted to start the day with a round of golf, so could I meet him at a golf course with his son and grandson for a round of golf? I told him I would happily meet some of my second cousins.

OCTOBER 27, 2014

I drove to Edgewood, Washington, and met my cousin Jerry Sinay and his son, Curtis, and grandson. We played golf at a local public golf course and did what all Sinays do; we laughed. We laughed until we cried over the silliest of things. There was no one out there serious about how they were playing golf. It was an enjoyable morning, and afterward, we went to a brother's house for a day of celebration. The brother's name was Keith, and he and the family spread food like I had never seen before. Many second and third cousins and their spouses were at the party, and I was trying to tell them what I was doing on my trip. It was odd because the kids did not know much about their grandfather, Jerry's father, nor were they familiar with their great-grandfather, Andrew Sinay. There was a mixed reaction to learning more about the Sinay side of the family even though all of them at one time donned the name, and the boys carried it, yet they were unfamiliar with the history of the name. I shared the ancestry report with those interested and told several stories to anyone who wanted to listen. Four of his children were there: Keith, Curtis, Mark and Darlene. Absent from the party were Kelly and Debra. I would meet Kelly at another time, but it was in the Irvine area when I visited a friend. In any case, it was just a fabulous party and tons of fantastic food and drink. I spent the rest of the afternoon there and learned about their lives and what they were doing with them. Several of the children of these brothers and sisters were there as well, and they were as fun to talk to as the rest of the clan. What I learned about the family was that they were a house divided politically. Some were supporters of Democrats, and some were supporters of Republicans. Although politics was not discussed at the party, one of the sons let me know how he was affiliated, and he told me. He also indicated that others did not feel the same way he did.

There is a short story by Edgar Allan Poe called "The Fall of the House of Usher." In his early description of the house, Poe indicated a barely perceptible fissure was running from the top of the house to the basement. The house was cracking, perhaps like the hero in the story, Roderick Usher, who was going mad. This is a crazy way of saying that a 'fissure" also exists in American Society, which is the ugly division we have in this country over politics. It is cracking our country apart, and the fissure in our house is getting wider. Will America survive? I am having doubts.

OCTOBER 28, 2014

The next day, I drove from Seattle to Lake Oswego, Oregon, to see a cousin from my dad's family. His name is Doug Sinay, the son of William Sinay and his wife Guernille. He was working while I visited him. He works in a cigar shop, and it is a smoking room for cigar smokers. We had much fun discussing the past, our parents, and our family history. I thought it was important that his sons know their ethnic background and where their great-grandfathers came from. I spent several hours with him at the shop and conversed with all the guys who came to smoke beautiful cigars. Doug shared stories I had never heard before, which is what it is all about. It was all about what he saw about our family history and what I had learned about it to tell him. I left satisfied that we had connected and learned much about our fathers and grandfathers. Thanks, Doug, for being so welcoming.

OCTOBER 28 AND 29, 2014

I left early in the morning to get to Bandon Dunes, Oregon to play two of the four courses (actually 5, with one being just a 13-hole course). I had a two o'clock tee time to play Bandon Dunes, the first course built in the area in 1999. Architect David McLay Kidd, an unknown in the golf architect world, designed it.

Getting around the complex was quite confusing, and it took me a while to figure out where to go. I arrived in time to grab some lunch and get to the golf course for my tee time. I arrived at the clubhouse, and there was no one to take the clubs from the car. It was not impressive. I got to the golf shop and paid my fees, only to realize there were no golf carts, but everyone must walk the golf courses. It seemed okay since it appeared that the courses were flat. There was no one else around, so the pro said I could tee off anytime I was ready. There was no range near the golf course. If I wanted to hit balls, I would have to drive to the range to warm up. That was, big time, ridiculous to me.

I put my golf clubs on the handheld golf cart and played Bandon Dunes. The course went straight out to the ocean and straight into the wind. The wind picks up in the afternoon, but I would learn that the wind is there in the morning as well. I was happy to play in the wind because I hit a low ball, and keeping it low was important. I played from the Green Tees, which were 6221 yards, but they played like 6600 yards because of the wind. I banged the ball around and enjoyed the beauty of this course, described as a cross between Pebble Beach and Carnoustie with a touch of Pine Valley. Those are some heavy comparisons since I had yet to play any of those courses and take their word for it.

BANDON DUNES GOLF COURSE IN BANDON, OREGON

The trouble with the course was not the walking, not the gorgeous beauty of it, but the wind was horrific. Although they claim this to be a great golfing experience, it depends on the strength of the winds. Even professionals have to struggle playing golf in the wind, and the more severe the wind, the greater the challenge and the less enjoyable the game. There is a particular kind of shot that golfers exercise in the wind called a knockdown shot. The player takes an extra club or two, places it in the back of the stance and swings it low by finishing low with the hands at the end of the swing. I hit knockdown shots all day, and they were effective, except the winds were so brutal to measure. Sometimes, the wind was a "three-club wind," other times, it was a "two-club wind," so it was a struggle around the golf course.

In addition to that difficulty were two other problems. First, the terrain was way more complex than one can imagine. It was just hell dragging a cart with the golf clubs barely hanging one in the wind. Some of the elevations to the holes were quite challenging. Secondly, the course could be more precise when deciding where the next tee box is. Oddly, there is a guide for golfers who get "lost" on the golf course! In all my golfing life, which has spanned fifty years, I have never seen a guide on a golf course to tell the golfers where the next tees are. And the guide is there in case some golfers have a cardiac arrest. Now, that was quite encouraging! Not knowing how difficult it was just to walk the course, much less drag a cart around, it was an unpleasant surprise about playing golf in this region.

Without repeating the narration of my round for Pacific Dunes, it was the same experience at nine o'clock the following day. It was just as windy and difficult to walk because of the wind. It makes the costly two rounds of golf quite a disappointment. One is sure not to enjoy the golf if the winds are significant, and I was told by one of the pros that the wind blows there all the time and that it is just a matter of how hard it blows. The marketing for these golf courses is clever, but I can guarantee everyone that playing Bandon Dunes is unlike playing St. Andrews, which I played in the wind and rain and still shot in the 70s. Bandon Dunes golf courses are a two or three-club wind all the time. It is rare for the wind to be still right on the Oregon coast.

I shot in the mid to high 80s in both of my rounds, primarily because of the problematic winds. It was unpleasant and physically challenging golf. Playing these courses at over two hundred dollars a round is incredible. It made eating lunch in the clubhouse unpleasant because I was exhausted playing golf. It was more like getting punched in the gut by Mike Tyson for thirty-six holes.

OCTOBER 30, 2014

I left Bandon Dunes on my way to Prospect, Oregon, hoping to meet with another cousin, John Orzeck. John is the oldest son of my mother's sister, Julia Labak Orzeck, one of my sweetest aunts. I got to Prospect around noon but could not locate John on his property. The neighbor next door asked me to come in and wait for him because he would come back in a short time. However, he did not come back, but we did spot his sweetheart in the front yard, so I drove onto the property, and she thought I was an intruder. I introduced myself and told her I was John's cousin. She told me he would be home later that night and that John would call me. When he called, he was kind and happy to hear from me. He then offered to come down from the hill and meet me at the hotel in Medford. Both John and his significant other, Ming, showed up right on time with these beautiful smiles. We hugged when they came through the door. We instantly had a great rapport, which improved as the night went on. We ate Chinese food, then returned to my hotel room and talked until 12:30 in the morning.

To summarize our conversation would be impossible, but to say that I had learned something would be an understatement. There used to be a radio newscaster who would tell a story at the end of the news and delay, which he was talking about the whole time. It might be a story about Thomas Jefferson or Ben Franklin. He would tell the listeners facts about the person, and each fact got more and more impressive as the listener listened. He was brilliant at delaying who he was talking about. At the end of the story, he would say who the person was that he was talking about, and then he would say, " And now you know the rest of the story."

My cousin John Orzeck is the oldest son of my mother's sister, Aunt Julia. He went to Occidental College on a four-year football and baseball scholarship. He was recently admitted to the Occidental College Hall of Fame for his participation and achievements as a football and baseball player. Great athlete. Anyway, he is a cousin I spent much time with during college and after college.

I learned from John "the rest of the story" about my grandparents on my mother's side and their children's lives. It was fascinating and engaging, and I grew to understand much more about how we become what we become. This happens to us because a little wizard pulls the levers behind the screen. I cannot divulge the content of the talks that we had because they are family secrets and they are family problems. What I did learn was that every family has some sort of problem that invades their lives and becomes the guiding principle in their lives. I leave the reader with this: Life sometimes deals with things we never thought would ever happen, and they happen because the man behind the curtain is pulling the strings.

I could not see their house because they did not want me to see it. They were hoarders of all the trinkets they had sold to soldiers on army bases up and down the coast of Oregon, California, and Arizona. They made their living that way. I had a great time with them, but found the whole experience with them to be ethereal.

OCTOBER 31, 2014

Before I left Medford, Oregon, I met with another cousin in Medford named Tricia Labak Golden. Tricia and I connected on Facebook through her sister, Gloria Labak Gewelke. Tricia and I had already had an hour or so conversation on the phone a month or so ago, and then we became connected more specifically through Facebook. What she and I had in common that I did not have in common with many of my cousins was a passion for the truth and an understanding of where the family name of Labak came from. Tricia had done her serious investigation some time ago, and I was working with ancestry.com as I was on this trip with a specialist to find out the details of my mother's parents and grandparents.

Meeting the cousins after all these years, and after all of our parents have died, has been quite interesting. Tricia shares my enthusiasm to leave a legacy of details for our children and their children to see on ancestry.com, as it will be there perpetually. I want my grandson to see his great-great-grandfather, great-grandfather, and grandfather in separate videos at different times over the last seventy-five years posted on ancestry.com. It will be quite a treat for him and my granddaughter to see them when they are adults, and want to explore an understanding of their family history. It is a gift I want to leave them, and this book is part of that. I still have work to do on it.

Today, I spent five hours with Tricia Labak Golden, and the hours just flew by as we were engaged in a unique and excellent conversation about family, inheritance, memories, and pictures. As I discovered, Tricia was born in 1955, and I am so proud to say that she was born the same year that Disneyland opened. I asked her what day Disneyland opened, and she did not know, so I told her it opened on my seventh birthday, July 17th, 1955. We gave each other a knuckle bump as we found ourselves bonded by our passion for the truth of our grandparents and that we are Disney-connected. What a coincidence.

Anyway, I found Tricia engaging, intelligent, and aware of what has happened with her family and what we both independently learned about our grandparents. She is going to help fill the tree (I hope) with some beautiful pictures of the family at different stages of their lives. She even gave me a particular picture of the family when they were all together. It is a fantastic picture and will surely be in the photo section of John Labak, my grandfather on my mother's side. Tricia was fun, funny, intelligent, passionate, and insightful. I loved being with her. It was interesting to see the characteristics of her that I have myself. It is incredible how I can see these characteristics in a woman I have never met until today. When I was growing up, she was seven years younger than me, so I had no memory of ever playing with or seeing her.

We had a wonderful lunch at a Thai restaurant and then returned to her house to say goodbye. It was so much fun in such a short period. It is too bad that I had never had the pleasure of being around her life at other times. This brings me to the thought that family has moved more and more away from one another over generations. Families used to be concentric, sharing times in the same city and having full family reunions. My parent's generation used to have many family reunions, and we all had fun playing with our cousins our age. As the cousins spread out and had their children, the connection disappeared. Despite the desire of the last generation for us to continue our reunions, there is no one making the effort to get the many cousins together and share the stories of their lives. So, the ancestry tree is the next best thing. I am trying to get them to put pictures of their families and let everyone else see whatever became of that cousin I remember as a teenager. I left Tricia at three o'clock and had a five-and-a-half-hour drive to Napa, California.

I felt this incredible feeling as I crossed to California from Oregon. Ah, back in the home state again, at last. The beauty of the state was immediately apparent. The mountains one travels through from Oregon to California are one of the prettiest parts of the country. I found the highways to be the best so far that I have traveled the entire country. However, I stopped and found gas higher than I paid in any other state. Yes, I was back in California, but I was still happy about it. While I drove south, I looked to the right and saw the sun setting. There it is, the California sun, the Sunshine State. Too much sun could also be harmful, and water will be a significant problem unless we get more rain. Now that I was back, I turned on the news, and they told me it would rain for the next two days. What timing?

So now the sun was on my right, not in my mirror, and I attempted to take pictures of the sunset. I got some good ones.

NOVEMBER 1, 2014

I stayed in the wine country area for five days, explored the area, and did as the Romans did when in Rome. I went to drink wine. My first winery was taken from a suggested article on the Internet because the article said this was a wonderful place to have a picnic lunch. It sounded good to me, so I went to Sattui Winery, which has been given many awards for its wine. I ate a ham sandwich for lunch, then went to the wine-tasting room.

The whole experience is about the wine taster getting you to join the club winery. The wine steward is a game to get you on their dole. Here is how it works: You join the club, and they give you a discount on the wine; however, a customer must buy two to three bottles monthly. That is fine if one is a wine drinker, but it is a waste of time if one drinks little. I passed on the opportunity but enjoyed talking to the young lady trying to "sell" me the membership. She gets paid more money if she sells a membership. I told her I just do not drink that much wine.

I do not. I enjoy it when I do, but I do not want the trouble if I am to pay for three bottles of over-priced (even at a discount) wine. Buying at the grocery store is more accessible when the wine goes on sale. I enjoyed tasting several wines but thought they could have been better. I thought they were average.

Moreover, they were overpriced. People who go into a winery like that and pay twenty-five dollars a bottle for the wine must be out of their minds. There is so much good wine out there for cheap and much less than at a winery that says, "We do not sell it outside of this store." I thought, "Why would you want to limit yourself like that when that is not even good business." They rely on the memberships that people get tired of after a while, but there are always fresh recruits. It is like selling a time-share only on a smaller level. I think one has to keep the membership for six months minimum.

After Sattui Winery, I took a stroll down the road to Chandon Winery, where they sell the bubbly Champagne. They have a big, expensive building where they have the wine tasting like one is getting special treatment. Not long after arriving, the wine steward pulled out the membership application like the other winery. This is what they are selling. You get to taste wines for the price of a bottle of wine (about 15-20 bucks), but you do not even get a bottle of wine. They make money on you tasting the wine! Then, they push the memberships. They always have these sexy women behind the bar smiling at you like you are the best since sliced bread when she wants you to join the club. I had to ask her how many bottles of Champagne she thought one could drink. They want to ship three bottles a month. I have not drunk three bottles in three years or more. Too many bottles, I told her, so I would not join the club. She quickly shifts her attention to someone she can sell to, so it is only a short time before you are dead meat there, just sipping on a glass of wine and enjoying the view. Fortunately, there were a few people that I talked to and found out what a small world it is.

When I got to Napa late the next night, I was putting things away in the hotel room, and when I finished, I got in the room and thought I felt the earth move. I thought I needed to sleep after a long drive to Napa. I did not give it another thought. Today, after the wineries, I went downtown to Napa and visited the area along the river. I saw a ghost town. I just needed to understand why there were so few people downtown. So I walked into an art gallery and asked the person inside, what is happening here in town? She said, "Dude, it was the earthquake on August 26th, and this place has not been the same. She narrated how severe it was, a 6.2 magnitude, and all the details of what happened to the city's older buildings. They were all condemned, as were new buildings that did not stand up to the earthquake. It was a severe and violent shaker. I remember reading about the earthquake in Pennsylvania, but I did not recall it when I came into town.

California is getting hit from all angles. We have had many fires, no water, and earthquakes. It is the price we pay for living in the land of the sun. We do not need a significant disaster in this state, but some rain. Does anyone want to do a rain dance?

NOVEMBER 2, 2014

It was a rainy day, so I took my time getting out, and someone did a rain dance because I never did. It was good, though, a good rain, but after a while, it dissipated. After a beautiful breakfast of Blueberry Pancakes at Alexis Baking Company Café, I went to see the neighboring towns and started in Yountville. Yountville is a small town, neat as a pin, with many cute shops and crazy good food. I liked Yountville—a nice community center with a great basketball court and many beautiful buildings everywhere. I ate lunch at Napa Style in the MarketPlace, a charming place. I took pictures of their artwork around the town and some trees near the community center.

While walking through the shops, I discovered an art studio, and while walking through it, I started seeing the work of a photographer named Dennis Hogan. I took a picture of his biography, and I thought he was nowhere near, so I started "oohing" and "awing" about these pictures of Napa Valley and how spectacular they were. I just loved them. Apologies to Don Lyons for saying I found his equal, but this guy had some unreal photos that were printed. They were pricey at $1,500 to 10,000 dollars for one of his pictures. So, while saying all these nice things, the guy said, "I am Dennis Hogan." Whoops! He was such a nice man, and we discussed the times, time passing, education in America, and living life. Cool guy. However, I told him I would consider buying one of his photos later.

I then drove to St. Helena and walked around town, but I did not find it all that interesting. I did not see what I was supposed to see, so I left without taking any pictures except the ones in my head. Instead of going on to Calistoga, I drove back toward Napa and stopped at a random winery.

I stopped at Laird Family Winery and enjoyed some whites and reds. I thought the wines were better than Sattui Winery in St. Helena, recently named the "Winery of the Year." One wonders how political and economic the decision for that title is. I did not find the wines there any better than at this Laird Family Winery, which I thought were even better than Sattui. It does make me wonder. Anyway, the guy at Laird spoke "wine language" like everyone has the same knowledge of the soils and the air and the location of the wine grapes. No matter what subject, everyone has a different level of knowledge about the subject. Speaking this "wine language" is why people can be easily fooled when told things they are unaware of. I let him talk.

I listened to a Great Course, "The Everyday Guide to Wine," by Jennifer Simonetti-Bryan, Master of Wine and Certified Specialist of Spirits. She is one of two hundred people in the country who can pass a master of wine tasting test that is extremely hard. Anyway, I listened to the tapes twice and learned a great deal about wine, but of course, I am no expert. I love eating cheese and crackers with wine. It makes the experience savor and cleanses the palate to enjoy the wine better. I used to ask my students who complained about an assignment, "Do you want a little cheese with that whine?" Most teachers have that phrase handy for their giggly students. The timing of it has to be correct, in any case.

What I do want to say is what I used to teach my kids in school. When you think you know a lot, then think of an iceberg. An iceberg has just a portion of its body poked out of the water. The mass of the iceberg is still below water. Your knowledge of a subject may equal the tip of the iceberg when others know almost the whole iceberg. These people usually have a Ph.D. They know much about the subject, and their knowledge goes down deeply into the water and nearly covers the entire iceberg. In other words, if you think you know something, you do not know what you do not know. Wine is a subject that has a great deal of information to learn, and it covers many areas: the land, the soil, the air temperature, the minerals in the soil, the grapes, and all sorts of things. The knowledge goes on and on and on. One can spend much time learning the subject and still figure out what to know. Sometimes, being a true expert in a subject can take a lifetime. So, what do we know? Depends. How much have you explored about any subject? It is why I can have nine lifetimes and still not have enough time to explore all that I want to know.

Taking pictures of Yountville brought to mind that one can take photos of a place at four different times: spring, summer, fall, and winter. So, one can experience a place in four different ways. Going to a location means I can enjoy what is in that particular season, but there are other seasons to enjoy. I will climb high on a hill tomorrow to enjoy a valley view. It is supposed to be colorful and different from any other time of the year.

PART 8

SONOMA, CALIFORNIA
TO INDIO, CALIFORNIA

NOVEMBER 3, 2014

Today, I met with Catherine Clemens Sevenau. Catherine and I went to the same high school, discovered each other on Facebook, and spent the day together, having an incredibly wonderful time. The short itinerary of the day included a tour of the town of Sonoma, lunch at the Kitchen Hotel Restaurant, a look at the town from a distant hilltop, a visit to the home of Jack London, and a great dinner at the Olive and Vine restaurant in Glen Ellen.

While touring the town, we happened upon a town bookstore. What do you think we saw in the window of the bookstore? It was Catherine's new book, *Passages from Behind These Doors: A Family Memoir,* with a note lying near the book indicating anyone interested should come to a book signing and a reading by the author on Thursday the 13th of November. Catherine then ran into the bookstore owner, who did an impromptu planning for the reading from her book. We then walked around town and chatted while dipping in and out of shops of various sorts. The town was lovely. It was a town square with a park in the middle and the town city hall in the middle. It is a pretty town and a cozy place to find a few glasses of wine. We must have walked by a dozen wine shops to do some tasting. Eventually, we ended up in the Sebastiani Winery, where Catherine ran into some friends. I saw some pictures of the barrels of wine in the winery—a very nice place.

After a short rest at home (we had walked to the town), we drove to the hills to get a view of the town from the hillside. It is a lovely setting and a perfect idyllic area. We discovered we had a mutual high school friend in the area: Scott Horine. Scott was on the basketball team in our senior year. He and I had much fun the summer before our senior year. Anyway, Scott was involved with wine distribution in the Sonoma area. Learning that Katherine had known Scott for some time was fun—small world.

We then went to the town of Glen Ellen, where there is a state park with a museum for the works of Jack London. It was fabulous to see how productive he was in his short life---he died at 40. Jack was a novelist and short story writer in the naturalistic literary movement. His novel *The Call of the Wild* was a high school reading requirement. The environment determines a person's fate, and Jack's stories perfectly reflect that. In our high school days, these stories were called Man versus Nature stories. It was not identified as the conflict of the story. We were dumb in those days. I was amazed at the house he had built on the property we visited, Wolf House, where he did not get to live. It was not completed before his death from gastrointestinal uremic poisoning. It does not sound like an excellent way to go.

The day was terrific. Catherine was one of the most excellent people I have met in a long time. She was fun, funny, intelligent, friendly, and a joy to be with for the day. I don't mean it that way; she would be a delight any day. I can't thank her enough for taking the time to make my visit to the Napa/Sonoma area to be such a fond memory.

NOVEMBER 4, 2014

I left Sonoma with a bit of sadness. It was a wonderful place, but I got an invitation to visit my cousin Deborah Sinay Wills in the Nevada City/Grass Valley area, and since I had not seen her for 40 years, it was terrific that I could see her. As the reader may recall, I met her brother, Doug, in Oregon and will meet her sister in Novato, California. When I arrived, she was the same young lady I had known as a teenager and still the vibrant and cheerful person I knew then. Deborah and I hit it off, and we just talked non-stop for hours, barely taking time to eat. We could talk and feel supported by what we said. We related life stories to each other. After the life stories, we turned to the family and all the aunts and uncles, and I shared what I had learned about them throughout my travels. She was a highly interested participant. Telling her the details of our grandparents and then a long discussion about our parents filled the time rapidly.

She wanted me to see a few things before I left. First, we visited where her former husband, David Wills, lived. I have a few pictures of where he lived and where he was about to build a house on the side of a hill, sort of Frank Lloyd Wright style. I looked at the elevations of the property he was about to build, and it was a clever design. I learned in my travels that people love to live in the city, those who love to live in the country, and those who love to live in isolated places. David liked it isolated. We discussed *Walden* by Henry David Thoreau, and I indicated that it might be a good idea once he is settled to take in the book while residing in the woods—the area had that Thoreauvian feel about it. It was a magnificent setting. Natural mushrooms grew around in the area.

After visiting David, we went to Nevada City, a charming turn of the 19th century town where Mark Twain stomped around when he came to Nevada during the Civil War. It was a pretty town, so we grabbed some ice cream and walked the town with Lily, Deborah's adorable dog. She also had two cats, Lola and Esther, that I bonded with at her house. They were all fun. After Nevada City, she drove us to Grass Valley, another delightful town with a 19th-century charm. There was a hotel where Mark Twain stayed, and so I had to take a picture of that. In Grass Valley, we stopped at a wine-tasting venue and met a lady who grows some interesting Italian wine grapes. Wow, we both loved them and grabbed a couple of bottles for dinner.

We went back to her house. We sat down with some great cheeses and those Italian bottles of wine and went deeper into the conversation about life, living, working, marriage, and many other topics. I found Deborah to be engaging, intelligent, insightful, and lively. I loved talking to her. Through the night, we rambled on and on until we had both exhausted ourselves, and the wine had gone from the bottles. We turned it in.

After a cup of tea, we dressed and ate breakfast in the morning. It was there that I told Deborah about details of the family from Slovakia that I had missed the night before—she was both shocked and amazed---another uncle who had died, a grandmother who had a child taken away, our grandfather's father-in-law born in the same city as my grandfather. It was all new information for her. It was all delicious. I appreciated that there was a cousin who cared enough to listen about the family history, letting her gain a bit more insight into who she was and where she partly came from. She never knew them; as I did, she felt a sense of completeness about family genes, behaviors, and traits. She drove me back to the house, and we said goodbye. Spending time with Debra Sinay was one of the most excellent times on my trip home.

NOVEMBER 5, 2014

I drove from Grass Valley to Novato, California, to visit the sister of the cousin I had just left. Her name is Claudia Sinay Mosias, and she is the oldest daughter of my Uncle Bill and Aunt Guernile. Uncle Bill was one of my favorite uncles, and he had a twin, Uncle Joe. They were not alike, and they were not identical, but they were fun, funny, and adorable uncles. I got to Claudia's house around two o'clock after spending an hour in the town of Novato just to see what it was like. Claudia and I immediately hit it off. She and I spoke on the same level and immediately started with the family. And we talked a great deal about the family name and all I had learned about the family history. Before long, her husband, Bruce Mosias, came home from a volunteer activity. He is retired, and Claudia still finds herself in the working world but plans a retirement next spring.

We found ourselves immersed in conversations about all sorts of subjects, and through dinner and into the night, we "covered the bases" of subjects and stories of family. During the evening and into the following day, I enjoyed the company of these two wonderful people. The depth of their discussion on various subjects was just fascinating and wonderful. I was beyond challenged and enjoyed the moments with them enormously. It seemed as if we had a great deal more to talk about even as I left.

I learned variations in interest in our family's heritage during my travels. The responses ranged from total non interest to total fascination with what I learned. Claudia ranks near the top in demonstrating an interest in when and where our grandparents were born, lived, and thrived. There are different levels of awareness of the importance of family history. There are different levels of interest in family history. I have nearly completed my journey and will have more to say in my final post.

To say that Claudia has a husband who is a wonderful guy is to understate the message. Bruce was about as good a listener as I have ever met. He engaged in the conversation with ease and enthusiasm. His contributions were insightful and significant. Learning what he does with volunteer work makes me feel guilty for not contributing more significantly to those less fortunate in my senior years. It is what I should be doing, and he has inspired me. I commend the efforts that he is making, however much he is making. We need to be a more selfless society; people like him lead the way. His time to learn to deal with those less fortunate or under challenging circumstances speaks volumes about his character. I enjoyed him as much as anyone I have met on my trip.

Finally, to my soul mate cousin, Claudia, I cannot believe we spent so much time apart and did not have more encounters. One has a special relationship with cousins that cannot be defined easily but has to do with a commonality of bloodline and characteristic thinking. Who knows what it is, but it is magical when one gets together with someone I have not seen in thirty years and can instantly connect on so many levels. There is a bond, which happens more so with those of the same age group. We are the same astrological sign and just one month apart in age. What a joy it was to talk to her, see another perspective of her family, and view what she saw as the family's oldest member. I found, too, someone who is just like me, a giver, not a taker in life. I found, too, one constantly aspiring to know another level of herself, another rung on the spiritual ladder of life. She reminded me of my sister in many ways: a giving soul who wants things to work out and dismisses conflict.

I took one picture of these two happy souls. I was privileged to share the half-day and the following day with them. They were very gracious, warm, and hospitable at their beautiful home. I cannot wait to join them in some place another time. It would be my distinct pleasure. Thank you again, Bruce and Claudia.

NOVEMBER 6, 2014

I left Novato, California, at 11:00 in the morning and drove to San Francisco. It was a spectacular day, so after checking into the hotel, I got out and walked to the harbor of San Francisco. That perception is funny, and we see things differently as the years go on. Even though I have been here several times before, it is as if I had not seen it the way I saw it today. It was better than I had seen it at any time ever in the past. I am trying to understand why. It is like reading a book: not what is in the book but what we bring to it improves the reading. What I have brought to San Francisco this time in the later years of my life makes it unique—I'm still trying to figure it out. I found a wonderful but highly commercial place with a high concentration on food. It is a lively place and has a spirit to it.

Seeing something aesthetically pleasing brings joy to one's soul and elevates the spirit. As John Keats said in his great poem, "Ode on a Grecian Urn." "A thing of beauty is a joy forever." Art never disappoints when it is great art. A city is a work of art, and I think San Francisco passes the test when one speaks of beautiful cities. I know that I overindulged in taking pictures, but they are the sites that I thought were interesting and stimulating, especially for my tummy. The city is just a thing of beauty.

Like other cities, San Francisco has those less fortunate, those I found wandering around lost and hopeless. I am going to do a unique page for them. I hope you enjoy seeing some places I have seen at various times. It is always a pleasure.

NOVEMBER 7, 2014

I saw two indigents in San Francisco who wandered around the city as if invisible. The guy on the left was singing with the musician playing in front of him. He looked like he was entirely out of it, either very drunk, high, or a combination. I watched him for a long time, and he was oblivious to my presence. He was into the song the musician was playing in front of him. I looked at this guy, and he appeared to be in his 40s, a good-looking guy, but obviously, things have not gone well for him. What got him to this point? Did he take his life and just trash it with drugs, and now this is where he is? To what degree does he represent the number of Americans who go so far in their lives as to "take" them by succumbing to drugs or alcohol? I am unsure what the statistics are about this problem, but I know it is not good. How is it that here in America, we have these normal-looking people bowing down to the distraction of drugs? What happened to them in life that brought them to this state of mind? Life can be challenging.

Another person, in this case, a lady off to the right, was just standing there talking to herself and talking to the air. Again, she was invisible to those around her, who just temporarily regarded her and then walked by. This lady has a mental illness but somehow falls between the cracks of what she needs to be to qualify for mental health care. Are we failing in this society to take care of the mentally ill? Are people like this just destined and resigned to wander the city streets and sing or talk to nobody? In my travels, I discovered that all cities have this problem and that the solution to this problem is not simple. Also, it is just not there. Are we a dysfunctional society that reflects the dysfunctional people we see on the city streets? Are we incapable of dealing with this problem? What are the people in Congress doing about it?

NOVEMBER 8, 2014

I spent the day on the Big Bus touring the city of San Francisco. I had never been on the Big Bus in San Francisco because it came here three years ago with its competitors. It was an excellent and fabulous introduction to a city I had visited many times before but seemed to spend only time in the Fisherman Wharf area. Now, with the Big Bus, one can see the city like you have never seen it before. I loved it. It is a more significant peak at the city and all of its history, along with the beautiful architecture that San Francisco has.

It was disappointing to see the number of homeless who lay around the city on the sidewalks, sleeping and dominating an area of the town where it would be uncomfortable to walk. It used to be a problem and still is to some degree to walk in the Haight/Ashbury area where there are too many panhandlers despite the efforts of the city to calm the panhandling down. When I got to the Wharf, there were panhandlers, and some were just pathetic. It was so pathetic that it was uncomfortable even wanting to give them some change. Although the city has done several things to decrease drug abuse and other problems, they have not yet decided to eliminate them from the avenue of tourists. It cheapens the city, and it makes it look worse than it is.

I know that problems like this are challenging to solve. These people are harmless to others, primarily to themselves, but unsightly in many ways. People who should not be doing the panhandling join the ranks, and then it becomes a game of deciding who gets the spare change and who does not. They even have religious people panhandling. Not very comfortable.

So much of the city has an incredible history; the defining moment was when the 1906 earthquake happened. It shaped the city, and it has become beautiful. It is a clean city with very little, if any, graffiti. I am just amazed at that, and there are no areas that are on display at any higher level than others. If it is there, they hid it from us. There is so much to explore here in the city, just like any other city, and taking a joy ride in it is just the tip of the iceberg when one wants to truly enjoy the city of whatever destination. It takes living in it to be able to enjoy it truly. What I did experience was the anomaly that the city is at this time of the year. It is warm in October and part of November, so I had two days of clear skies and 70-plus weather. It was just beautiful.

This is an example of how it can be that one experiences any place at different times of the year, and it is a different experience. Mark Twain mistakenly said, "The coldest winter I ever spent was a summer in San Francisco." It was something that people thought he said and he is attributed to do, but he did not. However, I have been there when I did not have enough clothing to care for how cold it was. I wore a short-sleeved shirt and a vest and was comfortable until five o'clock today. Despite the city's beauty, one does have to put up with some fantastic weather most of the time, and discouragingly during the summer.

I noticed many young people in the city, which is a testimony to the fact that they are expecting to move and live in the city before they want to move to the suburbs. Lots of mothers are pushing baby carriages around the city. It was a revelation.

I spent some time in Chinatown, went to get a lunch meal there, and was deceived. I hated that. Before I left, I told the owner I would write an evil report of the place because her worker stiffed me on the meal. It was a ridiculous thing to do. I will not detail it, but just take my word for it. She stiffed me. So don't go to Chinatown expecting to be treated like anything but a tourist. I disliked that a lot and ended up not spending any more money in that part of the city. I just did not feel I was going to get a deal. I felt I was going to get ripped off.

That did not spoil the day for me as I had a wonderful time in San Francisco, and I understand why they are so proud of their Giants. The city hall and the history of the city hall in San Francisco is one of the most exciting stories I have ever heard. It was supposed to be the capital of California, but it was politicized away from San Francisco to Sacramento. It should have stayed in San Francisco. The state would have been better served had it been in San Francisco. It has the best-looking capitol building in the country with several billion dollars worth of gold at the top, and yet, it is just the city hall. Interesting. I love the city. I will leave my heart there when I leave. It is hard not to fall in love with it.

NOVEMBER 9, 2014

After leaving San Francisco reluctantly, I drove to Palo Alto, California, near Stanford University. I hung out downtown and enjoyed a Mocha in Peets Coffee Shop, which has Wi-Fi. I spent the morning reading and biding my time before I met my last cousin on the trip. We were meeting at 1 o'clock. He resides in the town of Atherton, one of the swankier parts of Silicon Valley. My cousin Tim Oleno is the son of my Aunt Mary Sinay Oleno, the aunt who lived the longest in the family of eleven children. She was a ball of energy and only got slowed down when an accident broke her hip, an incident that was no fault of her own.

With his significant other, Mary Lou, Tim and I talked a great deal over the next several hours, and the time flew. I was so happy to be able to meet with them. While Tim prepared a snack, Mary Lou took me on a tour of the house and the yard. It was just a magnificent house built in 1904. The original things were fantastic, and the changes made over the years were incredible. It is amazing how people can live. I was so impressed with the house. She then offered us a family reunion at the house in the summer of next year. I said I would make a great effort to recruit people to come to the house for the reunion, and Tim offered to be my assistant.

Tim and Mary Lou traveled a lot and went to Prague the next year and to Slovakia. They also planned to go to Italy but would have been there before coming to Prague. Tim and Mary Lou were just as fascinated with ancestry as I was, and we talked endlessly about it. When I saw Tim, I was amazed at how much he looked like a Sinay even though he is only fifty percent Sinay, his father being an Italian. Some of the things that were particularly apparent in my search for the origin of the name Sinay were that those genes are so prevalent and dictate many different common characteristics and behaviors. It was a wonderful afternoon, and I had a wonderful time. They are super lovely people.

I then drove to my son's house in Los Gatos, and the kids and Brian had gone out for a walk. So I went out to find them, and Maeve, my daughter-in-law, said I would probably hear them just walking through the neighborhood. After a while, I found them. The kids saw me at the bottom of the street, and both came running to jump into my arms and hug me. They were both so cute. They just loved seeing Grandpa. We then walked along and talked as the kids played before us. James fell and scuffed his knee. He cried a bit but soon got over it—poor little guy. I told him I would put a good Band-Aid on it when we got home. I did.

When we got home, the kids had to get to bed, but James wanted to play catch with Grandpa, so we got him in his PJs and then played catch. James was very good at catching the ball from ten to twelve feet. He just loved doing it, and after a while, his Dad joined us, and we ended up having a hilarious three-person catch game. James was just fantastic. We ended that, and then James wanted to read to me. Ruth had to get to bed, so off she went. James then read me his favorite book. He read the whole book to me, and I could not believe how effective he was as a reader. He is just five years old, and he reads the whole book. He loved the book. Seeing how much progress he had made since the last time I saw him was so fun.

When James went to bed, Brian and I sat, drank some excellent French wine, and talked for about an hour. He told me they are selling the house and moving to Ireland. The reasons for this are long and difficult to relate in a short narrative, but Silicon Valley is too high-stress for the two of them. They can transfer to Google in Dublin and continue to work for Google. The house they will be able to buy in Dublin or near Dublin will not be as pricey as what they are selling, but the bottom line is that there is less stress in Ireland than here in Silicon Valley. Simple as that.

I look forward to visiting them and will see them more there than I do here. I will visit for extended periods and be able to golf on Ireland's great courses without paying for expensive hotels. So

I am looking forward to that. Tomorrow, I will go to the gym that Brian belongs to and hang out for the day as they have realtors showing the house by the dozens. There have been tons of realtors looking at the house already, and an offer is just days away.

NOVEMBER 10, 11, 12, 2014

The last three days have been a total joy, being with the grandchildren, James and Ruth, and their mom (Maeve) and their dad (Brian). We have been in non-stop motion, with one event after another to fill the day. In addition to what was happening, I spent much quality time with the kids, which all matters to me. I wanted them to know me a bit more, have fun with them, and then spoil them. So here are some of the things we did:

We went to the sports Basement sports store and bought James a baseball bat, a glove, and a few baseballs, and he then proceeded to take to it like a duck to water. The whole thing about him being able to catch a baseball at age five reminded me of the ending of the movie *Dr. Zhivago*. In the end, one of the girls, a child of Dr. Zhivago, can play the mandolin very well. The officer overseeing the new Soviet Republic said to the worker, "Then it is a gift." It was a gift from Dr. Zhivago's wife, Laura, who was also gifted at playing the mandolin. James has a great-grandfather who was an excellent baseball player, and his grandpa was not too bad himself, so it appears to be a "gift" from his ancestors. On the other hand, Ruth wanted a soccer ball and a pink football.

We played in the park on both Saturday and Sunday, and we played for nearly three hours. It was just fun and fun to watch them enjoy playing sports. James is particularly interested, but so is Ruth. She loved retrieving the ball for me. She tried to throw the ball, but a three-year-old has some learning to do. I was exhausted when all the playing was done and could not bend over. They ran circles around me. I so enjoyed it and laughed with them and at them all day long.

We had some excellent lunches and some very nice dinners, and Grandpa got to babysit for two nights. The kids were cooperative, and it could not have been easier. They honor what their mother and father expect of them. I fell asleep long before Brian and Maeve came home. It might be that Brian and Maeve will no longer need me to babysit the kids because the house they live in was also sold over the weekend. They have decided to move to Ireland and work at Google in Dublin. It is a big shock to everyone in our family. They needed to know why they were doing this; the lifestyle of Northern California was too stressful, and the traffic to and from work had doubled and tripled in the short time they moved to Los Gatos.

MY SON'S HOUSE IN LOS GATOS, CALIFORNIA

What can I say that will make life easier for them? Nothing. Life is a challenging series of choices, and one hopes to make them consistently well. I know they have a tentative plan, but they are still determining the outcome of their news. It is a bold move to sell a house and want a better outcome for them than they are currently experiencing. Given their work ethic, they will likely find a new way to keep things going positively. They have come so far already. It will be sad to see them leave this lovely town, but some things are not perfect, but then again, no place is perfect. For me, it was time to move on and play some golf in one of the best venues in the country: Pebble Beach.

NOVEMBER 13, 2014

I drove to Monterey early in the morning, just in time for my first round of golf at Spanish Bay Golf Course. This 18-hole course was designed by Robert Trent Jones, famed golf course architect, and Tom Watson and Sandy Tatum, both fans of British links golf. The golf course is listed in the top 100 most outstanding public courses in the country. Playing the course is always challenging, given that it has a high degree of difficulty. Although the course measures 6739 yards from the back tees, the weather can be an essential factor in playing the course. When it is windy, the course plays longer when hitting the ball into the wind. On the day I played, it was windy, so I chose to play from the White Tees, a distance of 6037 yards but a Slope rating of 131. The Slope rating is the degree of difficulty of the golf course. From the back tee markers of 6739 yards, the Slope rating is 143, a demanding course but not the most difficult by any standard.

For comparison's sake, let's assume we were playing Bethpage Black in New York. From the White Tees, the distance is 6704 yards with a Slope of 145. It is more complicated than Spanish Bay from the White Tees of Bethpage! The Slope from the back tees is 152. The maximum is 155. The highest in the country is from the back tees at the Ocean Course on Kiawah Island. It stretches to 7876 yards. It has a Slope Rating of 155. All of this is to show how different the difficulty of any golf course that one plays.

Spanish Bay had some outstanding golf holes, but it was not the best course I have ever played. From the White Tees, I managed a score of 82. It was the wind that made the round so tricky, and it would be the same for any course played in the Monterey Bay area. I found the course to be challenging because of the design, not necessarily because of the hazards. It was just not a fun design, but the day was beautiful, and the golf was always enjoyable no matter what the result.

NOVEMBER 14, 2014

My second round of golf was at Spyglass Hill Golf Course. I had played the course in the late 1980s but only remembered a little about it. I played with a mother and her son, and the son thought he would test the course from the back tees. Good luck, I thought. The course from the back tees is 7026 yards with a Slope of 145. That's pretty tough on an average day, but with wind, it would be a lot tougher. When a course is on the ocean, it is always windy. Today, it was slightly windy, but enough for a one-club difference. If I usually hit a nine iron from 110 yards, I might have to take an eight iron.

The round of golf was beautiful for me. I hit the ball straight and got up and down for par several times. I shot a good score of 79, and I was so pleased to break 80 on this course. The bomber I played with hit the heck out of the ball, but he wasn't always sure where it was going. On top of that, he could not put very well, and his score was in the high eighties by my calculation. Playing from those tees should be reserved for pros because even good amateurs will struggle with the length and the difficulty. His mother played a lot better than he did and scored well on several of the holes but had difficulties on some as well. We had a wonderful time.

When the pros play their tournament here in Monterey, they play three courses: Spyglass Hill, Monterey Ocean Course, and

Pebble Beach. The last round is played at Pebble Beach if you make the cut. If the weather is tame, the winner usually shoots 15 to 20 under par playing the four rounds or an average of five under each day. This is incredible golf, given how long and challenging these golf courses are: tomorrow, the beauty of them all, Pebble Beach Golf Course.

SPYGLASS HILL GOLF COURSE IN PEBBLE BEACH, CALIFORNIA

NOVEMBER 15, 2014

Golfing in Pebble Beach has been a dream of mine for many years, but I never had the opportunity to do so. I was so excited to play this course after watching the pros on TV play this tournament for many years. I was paired with two guys and a teenager. The two guys were decent golfers, and the teenager held his own. Jack

Nicklaus said that if he had one more golf round to play, he would do it at Pebble Beach. This was the best golf course he said he had ever played, and he has been all over the world playing golf.

I was nervous on the first hole but managed to hit a drive down the middle, but I chunked my second shot and did not get up and down for par. I took a bogey on the first hole. But after that, I settled down and did well. The two guys had a forecaddie, and when he saw that I could play, he told me where to hit my drives on each hole and where to aim. When I learned that, I felt much more comfortable and hit many of my drives right where he wanted me to. It was a beautiful day on the front nine, and I managed a score of 42 or 6 over par. Then the day turned dark and cloudy, and the wind came up for the back nine, but I was hitting the ball so well I managed a miracle 36 or even par on the back nine. I sunk a thirty-foot putt on number 18 to shoot even par. I hit one of the best shots of the day on 17 to about 12 feet of the pin, a shot the caddy said was quite reasonable given the wind conditions and the coldness in the air. It was a five-wood from 180 yards. Although I narrowly missed the putt, a tap in par nearly assured me of even par on the back side. I hit a good drive on 18, an excellent five-wood second shot, and had 130 yards to the green but the wind was blowing pretty well, and I came up short in the bunker but splashed it out and made the long putt for par. It was so thrilling to play this golf course and do well. The caddy took some great pictures and said he had never seen anyone do that well playing Pebble Beach for the first time. A 78 score was the highlight of my golfing career.

After the round, dinner in The Tap Room was just spectacular. It was a fun place, with golfers buzzing about their day playing at Pebble Beach. The day of golf was one of the best golfing experiences I have ever had. It was honestly so enjoyable, and it is hard to describe it.

During my golfing life, I played other courses in Monterey, including Cypress Point, one of the most exclusive golf courses in the country. Monterey Country Club, another prestigious golf club, and Poppy Hills Golf Course, a problematic but beautiful course for the public. Near the course of Pebble Beach is the miniature 18-hole executive course called The Hay, which has recently been renovated by Tiger Woods golf course team. I have yet to play the redo of that course, but it was a fun day playing that one the morning I left for home.

So these are nearly my last words from the trip, and I am sure some of you are "rotten glad of it" to steal an expression of Huck Finn at the end of *Huckleberry Finn*. I have also made a life journey like Huck and discovered so much about my family and the country. I have to bore you with one more writing to put an epilogue to this book I have written on this long journey around the country, meeting cousins and learning who I am in a final sense. And to finish some of the bucket list items I have always wanted to do. I am thrilled that I did them, and it has been such a pleasure to end the trip playing some of the best golf courses in the world. It has elevated my spirit.

**PEBBLE BEACH GOLF COURSE HOLE 18
IN PEBBLE BEACH, CALIFORNIA**

CONCLUSION

I took my last drive from Pebble Beach, California to Indio today, and I arrived home safely after having traveled 25,000 miles without a ticket, car troubles, or flat tires. I am most fortunate.

This has been an adventure, and I am thrilled I did it. My trip started with a visit to Melissa and Owen Larsen's place in Apache, Arizona, on May 3, 2014, and ended in Indio, California, on November 15, 2014. I have met quite a few of my cousins that I wanted to meet, and I have checked off some of the bucket list items that I wanted to see before I left this realm. I got a chance to see both of my children and their families. On my trip, I learned a lot of things about my extended family, and I learned as much about myself.

I learned that as far as families go, they all have problems and never escape the difficulties of being human. The usual family problems included work problems, estate settlement problems, sibling problems, genetic problems, money lending problems, retirement problems, generational differences, and the suspected parenting of the Greatest Generation. Some families had siblings who did not speak with one another, and some were families where all the siblings still had a healthy and friendly relationship. The dynamics of sibling relationships are one of the most complex things in life. No one understands why there is a black sheep in the family or why one goes off by oneself. It may be a part of natural selection and perpetuating the species. Who knows? I just know that it is indigenous to all families.

Each of these cousin families had their parents for different lengths of time, and there was no guarantee as to how long that would be. Life is what it is: unpredictable. Leaving this realm early is one of those unfair things in life. Some had their parents for the entire lifetime, and some for just half a lifetime. There was no telling. In the movie *Groundhog Day*, Life is one big crapshoot.

For those cousins who were so welcoming, asked me to stay with them, and treated me like family, I thank you enormously for your kindness. For those cousins who did not even respond to my pleas to see them, I feel disappointed with an understanding that life is still in their way to find time for a first cousin who just wanted to meet them and see how life was going. I understand it is difficult to call someone and ask them to see me on short notice, but it is difficult to predict when I will be in a given area when one is driving the country. So it was what it was, and I have no regrets for trying. For those cousins who met me and shared time with me, I am appreciative as I could put together the past and family history like I never knew before. It was gratifying to hear all your stories.

During my journey, I learned how vital heredity is to the influence of family. I learned that many of those who had those hereditary influences could not overcome them and even succumbed to them in one way or another. I saw the power of genetics as it worked in the family for and against people. It appeared that several people suffered "the slings and arrows of outrageous fortune concerning genetics, and they were not sure what was guiding their lives. It is not fate. It is not a choice. It is genetics. I say this because I know that my genetics are what I am personally up against. One never knows what they will dole out.

The variation in interest in the family name was staggeringly different and ranged from no interest to a high degree. However, it needs to be clarified what the impact has been and its importance to those who have learned a new history of their grandfathers and grandmothers. Perhaps someone in their down line will one day look at the work that I have done and say, "I think he was forward-looking, and he knew that one day this would be important to many people." For me, it was essential to get the message out and declare who our grandparents were so that succeeding generations could look at the website and see how they were and what they were like. For me, that has been everything.

I was so fortunate to be able to meet some great people along the way and to be able to circumnavigate the country without any unfortunate incidents. I was pleased to meet Mark Ritchie, an excellent host in Woodstock, Illinois, and a fun person to be with in Augusta, Georgia. I was also pleased to meet his friend Pat and recall our fun playing at Augusta Country Club. I was fortunate to play some of the best golf courses in the country when I played Louisiana TPC, The TPC Players Course at Ponte Vedra Beach, Augusta Country Club, and Oakland Hills North and South Course. These were some of the finest golf courses I could ever hope to play. I had a tremendous time playing them and meeting people on them, which enhanced the experience.

I learned a great deal about my country and a great deal about the history of this remarkable place. We Americans have a tremendous geographical place here on this planet. It is still a question as to how we will deal with the place we have as future generations become a part of the American fabric. I think our ethnicities are becoming so enmeshed that it is hard to distinguish one person's origins from another's. I saw a lot of ethnically diverse kids playing with each other in the cities, and we are going to be a country of a true melting pot of the world, a new American like we have never seen before. Our country is a beautiful playground with great national parks set aside for us and future generations to enjoy. It is a tribute to those who were forward-looking enough to do that: Teddy Roosevelt. This land is so much a country of farms; it is incredible how much our farms do for the rest of the country. It is quickly taken for granted. This country is so much a country of trucks and trains. They deliver for us every day of the week.

I discovered an American past that I did not care for and a past that has stretched its arm to today. The racism we practiced is still in full vogue today and will not improve. I've seen all the biased chuckleheads come out of the closet and show their ugly teeth to our current president, and they are not likely to help him accomplish anything. He is half white, remember? For that reason, I do not foresee a promising future. Although I lived through some difficult times in America, there are more difficult times ahead. Let's hope not for the sake of our grandchildren.

I was so glad to have traveled the country and gained a better perspective than I ever thought I would. It was an adventure I would think about for the rest of my life.

HOME IN PALM DESERT, CALIFONIA

A SHORT HISTORY OF THE ANDREW CHARLES SINAY FAMILY

The following is a short history I wrote from the research I received from ancestry.com. The research by ancestry.com is in Appendix B, along with the documents to back up the research of the Sinay ancestry. As an introduction to the findings by ancestry.com, I recommend reading my summary here and then reading the research by ancestry.com. After reading both writings, the reader should know what the ancestry people discovered about Andrew C. Sinay.

Andrew Charles Sinay was born on August 8, 1879, in Nagy-Saros, Saros, Hungary, and Velky Saris, Slovakia. He was illegitimate, so we do not know his biological father. He was born Andras C. Szinai to his mother, Zsuzsanna Szinai, a day laborer when she was 24. After one year, Zsuzsanna, born on August 2, 1855, in Bodlonlaka, Saros, Hungary, now Bodovce, Slovakia, married a German named Pal Swanzigar on May 17, 1880. He was 30, and she was 25. Together, they would have four children: Maria (1882), Janos (1884), Istvan (1887), and Anna (1889). They were all half brothers and sisters to Andras.

When I was in Canton, Ohio, in 1976, on my way to Europe, I stayed at Uncle Joe Sinay's house for one night. I had a friend with me, Tom Henley. As we sat and drank beer, the party got lively, and my Aunt Sue Seaman told a story about the origin of the Sinay name. She indicated that our real name was Swanzigar. I am sure she did not know how to spell it, but my friend and I just laughed when she told that story. We thought it was a hilarious story. Uncle Joe laughed like crazy, too. We were all drinking, and it just made the story seem so funny, and of course, it was funny then, but it was half true. The Zwanzigar name is material to the Sinay side only because the children she had with Pal are related to Grandpa as half brothers and sisters. He is not the father of Andras, our grandfather, but we will never know who that was. It is a German name because the distribution of the name only occurs in Germany today. The German Football (i.e.soccer) Association is named Theo Zwanziger, so it is safe to say he was German since the name also is 20 in German! How and where she met that guy is a mystery, but leave it to the speculation that she was a mover and a shaker, given that she had one child out of wedlock and then married out of her ethnicity when she did marry. The name Zwanzigar does not occur in Slovakian or Hungarian locations.

I point this out because the number of stories circulating in the Sinay family about our name and its origin were so diverse that, after a while, no one knew what to believe. When Aunt Sue told the story, it was obvious that she did not know that Grandpa Sinay was illegitimate. I am unsure if any children knew that Grandpa Sinay was illegitimate. Otherwise, it would have been understood, but my father never told me my grandfather was illegitimate. I don't think my father knew this; indeed, any of the uncles who took an interest in the Sinay family name would have shared this if they knew. To my knowledge, none of them knew this. Grandpa Sinay took his mother's name. Grandpa Sinay was named after his grandfather, Andras Szinai; Zsuzsanna's father has a Hungarian name and died in 1880, just a year after his grandson Andras C. Sinay was born. He was not at his daughter's wedding to Pal Zwanzigar, but her mother was there. Her name was Maria Novotny, a Slovakian name. Both

Andras and Maria were born in modern-day Slovakia, so it appears we are mostly Slovakian with a mixture of Hungarian. Zsuzsanna was born in Bodonlaka, Saros, Hungary, now modern-day Bodovce, Slovakia, on August 2, 1855.

There are distinct differences between Hungarians and Slovaks. The languages and customs and their backgrounds are of different origins. Just read this article to see what I am talking about: http://www.spiegel.de/international/europe/language-wars-frustrations-grow-among-slovakia-s-hungarian-minority-a-649443.html.

We all know that Grandpa Sinay spoke Slovak because I heard him speaking it to my mother in the kitchen when she was cooking and he was visiting. My mother was Slovak, so she did not know Hungarian. Grandpa could "get by" speaking some Hungarian, but I think he was comfortable speaking Slovak. Additional evidence of the origin of the Sinay ethnicity is the 1930 Census when Grandpa Sinay indicated that he was from Slovak land! Slovak land was the area in the north of Hungary. The area is still under dispute to-day, as you have seen if you read the article I posted in this narrative. In short, we are primarily Slovakian with some Hungarian mixed in on Grandpa's side. Szinai is a Hungarian name; one can see it in the phone books there. I searched LinkedIn and connected with Szinai's in Hungry and America. Some people came from Hungary and kept the Szinai name. One time, I met a colleague's husband, whose name was Hunsaker. I asked him what the origin of the Hunsaker name was, and his response was, the same as yours, Sinay, it is Hungarian! Yikes! I was a bit embarrassed, but he did tell me that Sinay (pronounced ES NAY in Hungarian) was a common name. So even though the surname Szinai is Hungarian, we ended up in the Slovakian camp and are much more Slovak than Hungarian. It is but the name that makes us part Hungarian. Ethnically, we are primarily Slovakian.

Grandma Sinay was born Rozalia Maria Almassy on August 28, 1880, in Kass, Abauj-Torna, Hungary, now Kosice, Slovakia.

Although her name is also Hungarian, she was born to Janos Almassy and Susanna Hnath. His name is Hungarian, and her name is Slovakian. He was born in the same town as Andras Szinay or Sinai. He was born on September 13, 1858, in Nagy-Saros, Saros, Hungary, or Velky Saris, Slovakia, the same town as Andras Szinai. He married Susanna Hnath, born in Ujak, Saros, Hungary, now Udol, Slovakia, on November 9, 1879. He was a miller's assistant. He was 21, and she was 35! She was a servant. They would have three children together! There was a story that Grandma's parents had a beer garden, but there is no evidence. They were simple people. There is no royalty in the family either, as there were rumors that Grandma came from royalty. If they had a beer garden, it is something we cannot prove, as there is no evidence of that in the records. Indeed, we know that Grandma was not of royalty. These were stories that were rumored around and had no basis in truth. Janos Almassy's parents were Simon Almassy and Elizabetha Drobnyak, again a Hungarian and a Slovakian name mixed. So, as we are proceeding backward in Grandma Sinay's lineage, it appears to be a mix of both, but the Slovakian side was dominant.

Grandma Sinay passed away on May 3, 1960. I was a server at the mass given for my Grandmother. I was just 12 years old, and my most vivid memory was a man who came in to give us money to serve the mass, and Father Krisco took it and said, "We have a fund that we keep for the servers." Oddly, we were never told about any fund. Five dollars to a 12-year-old was like gold in those days. We left for California in August 1960, so I never enjoyed any funds from my grandmother's funeral. I tell the story as a remembrance of the life of Rozalia Almassy, not to denigrate anyone or cast aspersions. An article in the Canton Repository on her passing indicated that she was born in Kosice, Austria. This is the correct city but the wrong country. She was born in Kosice, Slovakia, as I indicated. It also indicated that Rosalie was a First Catholic Slovak Ladies Union member. This is another indication that our Grandparents are Slovak and from Slovakia. We must remember that from 1914 to 1993, the country was Czechoslovakia, not The Czech Republic and Slovakia as it is today. She was buried in Calvary Cemetery in Massillon, Ohio. She is located in Lot 68 W ½, and I assume she is next to Grandpa. I will visit the grave when I make my visit to Ohio! It was told to me by Karen Anderson Hursh, wife of Greg Seibert, that Rosalie's Catholic Slovak Bible resides at St. Andrews Abby in Cleveland, Ohio. Also, baptism records for all our parents can be archived from St. Patrick's Church in Canonsburg, PA. The source for the records of Rozalia's birth and baptism were from Kassa Roman Catholic Parish in Slovakia. It was indicated that she had Hollo Zug Street #3 as her residence at birth.

Grandma Sinay had one brother and one sister. His name was Istvan or Anglicized into Steven. So we can understand why she named one of her children Istvan! I will tell his story in a bit. Istvan came to America with Grandma and went straight to Chicago. Here, he laid down the roots of a big Almassy tree, and I am happy to report that I have connected to one of your first cousins on that side of the family. He did not know that there was another set of families in Ohio. So, cousins, you have tons more first cousins (once removed) on the Almassy side! They are all in and around Chicago, where Istvan Almassy went when he came to America. Grandma's sister, Maria Anna, remained in Slovakia and lived there. I have no information about her. I do not know if she was married or what. Only so much can be done with the dollars you give to the genealogist. We have a birth certificate and a baptism record for her as she was born a year younger than Rozalia on December 25, 1881.

When Grandma Sinay came to America, she came on the Ultonia, a ship that departed from Flume, Croatia, and arrived in New York at Ellis Island on November 4, 1910. She arrived a year after Grandpa Sinay arrived on October 28, 1909, on the ship Blucher departed from Hamburg, Germany. When I was in Hamburg, Germany, in the 1990s, I did not know my grandfather had departed from that city to come to America. It was the same experience when I went to the tip of Long Island, New York, and saw the port of Southampton, where he had arrived a hundred years before. So I had trampled on the ground my grandfather had been on at some time. It is a small world indeed!

Grandma traveled with three children, but one would not make it to Ellis Island. Our Uncle Steven (Istvan) died on the Island of Hoffman at Hoffman Hospital on November 20, 1910, the hospital that quarantined kids with contagious diseases as they arrived in America. It would be traumatic for Grandma Sinay to lose a child upon arriving in America. This Island was made famous in <u>The Forgotten of Ellis Island</u>, a book about those children who never made it to Ellis Island because they died on Hoffman Island, the quarantine island for contagious people, primarily children. She did not know what was to become of him for at least 16 days after his arrival. He died of measles, diphtheria, and several other disorders on his death record. He is buried at Mount Olive Cemetery in Maspeth, New York. He is in grave 1547. He was ten months old. I have included him on the family tree for obvious reasons. He was one of the kids and one of those who died alone on Hoffman Island without his mother at his side. I did have Grandma tell me a story about Steven when I was a kid, but she had difficulty expressing exactly what she wanted to say, so I did not understand all that she was saying. I knew she was heartbroken about what had happened to him, and she most certainly never got over that. I am sure he would have been a great guy, just like all the other aunts and uncles I had on the Sinay side.

It was indicated on the shipping record that Grandpa Sinay was coming to America to be with his cousin Johan Durkac. His wife's name was Mary, and we are unsure if she or Johan was the cousin! I have not been able to establish that there is a relationship between the two. However, climbing on that tree branch was an additional cost, and I did not think it was as important as it was to find our true identity. I did pursue an exploration with a Slovakian genealogist, and he did not find a connection between Grandpa and Johan Durkac. There is still more to do on this tree, but I have devoted all the money I want to for this project. To be able to determine our rightful origin in the history of the Sinay name is well worth the money. Perhaps someone else will pick up that branch of the tree. I am including an invitation to visit the tree and check it out.

Grandpa Sinay died on December 13, 1967. He was at our house in California for some months in 1965 and was at the 25th anniversary of my mother and father, Andy and Ann Sinay. My mother took an 8 MM film of him walking in the front yard. It is a good movie of his, and I will upload it to the tree for everyone to view. Grandpa was 88 years old when he died. When he visited us at the house in Brea, CA, in 1965, I was a sophomore in high school. He came out of his room one day and started waving a piece of paper around, and he wanted to show it to me. I did not recognize the paper and thought it was his birth certificate. It was not. It was a naturalization certificate given to those who attended classes and passed an exam to indicate citizenship. He did not speak very well as he had had his larynx taken out due to cancer. On top of that, he was drinking from a whiskey bottle and liked chewing garlic. Wow! When I was a kid, I used to go to his house and work on the yard until the trimming was perfect. He gave us some crucial lessons on doing things well instead of poorly. He was demanding. I remember the vegetable garden he kept and the beautiful dishes Grandma made from garden vegetables. It was rare to have anything to eat there at her house. We did enjoy it, though.

When Grandpa came to America, I never learned what he did to earn a living. Although he was a tailor in Slovakia, he did something else when he first came here. He worked in the coal mines, but I am not sure. I know that they resided at 304 Elm Street in Canonsburg, PA. They left for Canton, Ohio, before 1925. The 1920 census lists the family as Sini, but the census taker wrote things down phonetically and needed to verify the family's last names better. On the census, it indicates that both parents were born in Slovak land and both spoke Slovak. We all know how important it was for Andras and Rozalia's children to marry their own "kind." Grandma Sinay chose my mother because my mother was Slovakian and Catholic, not in that order. It was important for the two of them to marry Catholics, and we know it was difficult for those kids who did not marry Catholics. They found themselves ostracized. It was not a good thing. I assume this is normal in a family of 12, especially when the dominant religion is Catholic.

When Grandpa Sinay moved to Canton, he went to work for the Republic Steel Corporation and had a long career there, but he may have had other jobs there as well. Grandma was a stay-at-home mom. Raising ten children through the Great Depression must have been quite a challenge. My dad used to say how little they got to eat when they were younger. Grandpa Sinay listed his father's name on the social security application as Paul Cvisgar. Grandpa did not know how to spell his stepfather's name. This added to the confusion of finding out his father's name. However, the application listed his mother's name as Susan Sinay. This application for a social security number was done on November 27, 1936. It is another validation that Grandpa Sinay took his mother's name.

So there is evidence of our ethnicity, which means a lot in the direction of being mostly Slovakian since both Grandpa and Grandma Sinay spoke Slovak and indicated this is where they came from. I am especially Slovakian, given that my mother's father and mother were also born in Slovakia—no wonder I love all the Slovakian food like Huluski and other dishes. I even have a Slovak cookbook. So there you are, cousins, a short history of the Sinay name. I am happy to put to rest all the mystery of the Sinay name. I hope you will share this with your families: first, your children and then their children so that if they are a part of the Sinay name, they can proudly say that it is a Hungarian name but that their grandfather, great-grandfather, or great-great-grandfather was mostly Slovakian. It would also apply to our grandmother in the same way. We have Hungarian names from both Grandparents, but we are primarily Slovakian.

I used to tell the story that my last name was spelled with a "J" at the end and was changed to a "Y." It was deceiving to read some of the American documents about our name as the 1920 Census had it Sini and Grandpa's naturalization certificate spelling our name with a "J." So, no wonder there was so much confusion aside from all the stories Grandpa used to tell and then how the children would repeat varying stories about the Sinay name.

RESEARCH REPORT FOR THE ANDREW C. SINAY FAMILY

This is the research report from ancestry.com on Andrew C. Sinay's ancestry. This detailed report justifies with complete research on where he and his wife, Rozalia, were born, where they married, and when they came to America. It was a painstaking task to rewrite this report, but it was necessary to share it with as many ancestors as possible. When the reader sees a number in parentheses after a sentence, it references a document that will follow this report.

RESEARCH REPORT: SINAY, APRIL, 2014

The objective of this research session was to determine the origins of the parents of Andrew M. Sinay, Andrew C. Sinay, and Roselia Almassy and locate them in the records of that place. The client has a tree on Ancestry.com entitled "Andrew C. Sinay Family Tree." The information in this tree was reviewed and used as a starting point. The client provided additional family information and historical records. These will be referenced throughout the report as they are relevant. For anyone who wishes to view the tree I created, please send me your email address and I will send you a link for you to have access to the tree.

GENERAL METHODOLOGY

Most of this research was conducted using the Roman Catholic and Greek Catholic church registers of baptism, marriages, and deaths for the towns where the ancestors came from. Some civil birth and marriage records were also obtained from the Slovakia State Archives in Presov, Slovakia.

In almost every historical record, before the family came to the U.S., the surname Sinay was written as Szinai. There was one exception where it was written in Szinay. The "i" and the "y" in Hungarian are interchangeable. The consonant "Sz" sounds like the English "s." So, they would have pronounced the name (phonetically) See-nah-ee. The name Szinai is Hungarian. The surname Almassy is also Hungarian. Both names can be found in the on-line phone and address directory for Hungary. The other surnames found in the pedigree (Novotny, Drobynak, and Hnath) are Slovak surnames. In all U.S. records, the Sinay family consistently reported their ethnicity as Slovak and their native language as Slovak. There was likely intermarriage between ethnically Slovak and ethnically Hungarian people earlier in the pedigree. The region where the ancestors came from was a part of the Kingdom of Hungary during the time of the Austro-Hungarian empire, and later became part of Czechoslovakia after World War I and is now part of Slovakia.

ANDREW CHARLES (ANDRAS) SINAI AND ROZALIA MARIA ALMASSY

Andras Szinai was born on 8 August 1879 in Nagy-Saros, Saros County, Hungary (now Velky Saris, Slovakia). He was baptized two days later. His baptism record (found in the Nagy-Soros Catholic church registers) says that he was the illegitimate child of Zsuzanna Szinai. His godparents were Gyorgy Demko and Maria Miscsink. Zsuzsanna Szinai was residing a house number 46 in Nagy-Saros. The client provided an abstract of the baptism record from Slovakia. (1) A copy of the original register was made from microfilm at the Family History Library. (2) There was also a duplicate copy in Latin found in the microfilms at the Family History Library, which is probably from the diocese records. (3)

Andras married Rozalia Maria Almassy on 3 February 1904 in Nagy-Saros. (4) Rozalia Maria Almassy was born on 28 August 18180 in Kassa, Abauj-Torna County, Hungary (now Kosice, Slovakia). She was baptized there on 31 August 1880. She was the daughter of Janos Almassy (born in Nagy-Saros) and Zsuzanna Hnath. The client provided an abstract of the Rozalia baptism record issued from Czechoslovakia in 1953. (5) This certificate incorrectly gave her mother's maiden name as Ujack. The original entry (copied from the microfilm at the Family History Library) shows that her mother's name was written as "Ujak Susanna Hnud (Saros)" in this record. (6) It is understandable why the registrar in Czechoslovakia who issued the abstract thought that Susanna's maiden name was Ujak. Hungarian surnames are always listed before first names, so the register gave the name written before Susanna as her maiden name. However, records for Rozalia's siblings (discussed later in the report) show clearly that she was Susanna Hnath and that she was born in the town of Ujak in Saros County, Hungary (now Udol, Slovakia). (7)

Andras immigrated to the U.S. in 1909. He departed from Hamburg, Germany, on 17 October 1909 aboard the ship Blucher (8). He arrived in New York on 28 October 1909. (9) In his arrival list, his ethnicity was given as Slovak, while his nationality was "Hungary." He was joining his cousin Johann Durkas in Cannonsburg. (Washington County), Pennsylvania. His nearest relative in Hungary was his wife Rozalia in Nagy-Saros.

Rozalia and her three children (Ilona, Zsuzsa, and Istvan) followed their father about a year later, arriving in New York on 4 November 1910 aboard Ultonia. (10) Rozalia's ethnicity was also listed as Slovak in this record. She was joining her husband, Andre Szinai, in Canonsburg (Washington County), Pennsylvania. Her closest relative in Hungary was her brother Stephen Almasi in Nagy-Saros.

Andras and Rozalia (Andrew and Rosie) were enumerated in the 1920 census in North Strabane Township, Washington County, Pennsylvania. (11) Here, Andres and Rosie's birthplace was "Slovakland," and their native language was Slovak. They moved to Ohio in 1925 (evidenced by the fact their daughter Dorthoy was born about 1925 in Ohio), and in the 1930 census, they were enumerated in Canton, Stark County, Ohio. (12) These two census records provide the names of their children in the U.S. after they immigrated. In all, it appears they had 11 children (if the census record accounted for all of them). The first three were born in Hungary, the others in Pennsylvania and Ohio:

1. Ilona (Alice) Sinay, born November 23, 1904 in Nagy Saros (13)

2. Zsuzanna (Susie) Sinay, born October 27, 1905 in Nagy Saros (14)

3. Istavan (Stephen) Sinay, born in 1909 and died November 20, 1910.

4. John Sinay (John)

5. Andrew M. Sinay (Andy)

6. Mary Sinay (Mary)

7. Emil Sinay (Emil)

8. Margaret Sinay (Margaret)

9. Joseph Sinay (Joe)

10. William Sinay (Bill)

11. Dorothy Sinay (Dorothy)

Andras applied for a Social Security Number on 27 November 1936. (15) His name was given as Andrew Charles Siany. He worked for Republic Steel Corp. in Canton, Ohio. His birthday was given (incorrectly) as 30 August 1879. His mother's maiden name was listed as Susan Sinay, and his father was Paul Cvisgar.

Andrew died on 13 December 1967 in Canton, Stark County, Ohio. He was 88 years old and widowed. Rozalia had died several years previous on 3 May 1960.

ZSUZANNA SINAI AND PAL ZWANZIGAR

As mentioned, Andras Sinai was born in 1879 to Zsuzanna Szinai. On 17 May 1880, Zsuzanna Szinay married Pal Zwanzigar in Nagy-Saros County, Hungary (now Velky Saris, Slovakia). (16) This marriage record was precious because it told that Zsuzanna was 25 years old (i.e., born about 1855), was born in a place called Bodonlaka, and her parents were Andras Szinay (deceased) and Maria Novotny. Interestingly, Pal's place of birth is said to be "unknown."

The children of Pal and Zsuszanna Zwanziger found in the Nagy-Saros Roman Catholic church baptism registers were

1. Maria Zwanziger, born January 29, 1882, was baptized on February 2, 1882.

2. Janos Zwanzigar, born September 27, 1884, baptized September 28, 1884.

3. Istavan Zwanzigar, born January 7, 1887, was baptized on January 9, 1887.

4. Anna Zwanziger was born on June 19, 1889, and baptized on June 23, 1889.

Zsuzanna's baptism record was found in the registers of the Szenthyorgy Roman Catholic parish (now Hubosovce, Slovakia), the parish to which Bodonlaka belonged. (21) Zsuzanna was born on 2 August 1855 in Bodlonlaka, Saros, county, Hungary (now Bodovce, Slovakia). She was baptized the next day. Her baptism entry gives her parents' names as Andreas Szinay and Maria Novotny. They lived at house number 15 in Bodonlaka. There was not enough time to locate Zsuzanna's sibling and her parent's marriage record, but this could be done in a future session.

JANOS ALMASSY AND ZSUZSANNA HNATH

As mentioned, Rozalia Almassy was the daughter of Janos Almassy and Susanna Hnath. Janos Almassy was a miller by occupation. He was initially from Nagy-Saros, Saros County, Hungary (now Velky Saris, Slovakia). Susanna Hnath was originally from Ujak, Saros country, Hungary (now Udol, Slovakia).

Rozalia was born in 1880 in Kass, Abauj-Torna County, Hungary (Now Kosice, Slovakia). Kass was (and is) a large city, so searching page-by-page through the baptism registers could be very time consuming. Using an index to Roman Catholic baptism records on

FamilySearch.org, another sibling of Rozalia was found in Kassa: Marian Anna Almassy, born 25 December 1881 and baptized 1 January 1882 in Kassa; the family residence was 15 Nagy-Ludmar Street in Kassa. A second sibling was found using the Family Search.org indexes. This was for Ludwig Istvan Almassy, born 14 August 1886, baptized 22 August 186 in Iglo, Szepes, Hungary (Now Spisska Nova Ves, Slovakia0; family residence; house number 145 in Iglo. (23) In the section for remarks, the priest noted that Istvan married Anna Csanda in Nagy Saros on 28 May 1911. A request was made to the Velky Saris registration office for this marriage record. They will not provide a copy, but they did provide an abstract of the marriage:

> Marriage: 27 May 1911 in Nagy-Saros
> Groom: Istvan Lajos Almasi, Roman Catholic / church, born 14 August 1886 in Nagy Saros,
> Father: Janos Almasi; mother, Zsuzanna Hnat
> Bride: Anna Csanda, born 10 October 1892 in Nagy-Saros, father of Andras Scanda, mother Erzebet Mihalik
> Witnesses: janos Pasztor, Andras Gazsik

The client knew about the sibling, Ludwig Istvan Almassy. He also immigrated to the U.S. On 24 November 1936, he applied for a Social Security Number. (24) In this application, he gave his parents' names as John Almasy and Suzanne Knapp. Knapp must have been his Anglicization of the surname Hnath. Janos and Susanna Almassy likely had additional children, but no others were found in the online indexes for baptisms. Additional searches in the records on microfilm could be done in the Roman Catholic church for Kassa and Iglo. This could be pretty time-consuming since Kass was a large city.

If Rozalia were the firstborn child, then Janos Almassy and Susanna Hnath would have likely married sometime before 1880, probably between 1876 and 1880. They could have married sometime before 1880, probably between 1876 and 1880. They could have married in Kass (where Rozalia was born), in Nagy-Saros (where Janos was born), or in Ujak (where Susanna was born). Roman Catholic church marriage registers for each place were separated beginning in 1880 and working backward, and their marriage was not found. Their marriage was ultimately found in the Eperjes Greek Catholic church registers, the parish to which the Greek Catholics in Nagy-Saros belonged. (Eperjes is known today as Presov, Slovakia). (25) They were married on 9 November 1879. The marriage record shows that Janos was 23 years old, a miller by occupation, Roman Catholic, and born in Nagy-Saros. Susanna was 35 years old, a servant by occupation, Greek Catholic, and born in "Eperjes Ujak." Unfortunately, their parents's names were not given in the marriage record.

The marriage record says that Janos Almassy was 23 years old in 1879, indicating that he was born about 1856/1857. A baptism record was found for him in the Roman Catholic church registers for Nagy-Saros. (26) This indicates that he was born in Nagy-Saros on 13 September 1858 and baptized the next day. Even though his birth year is a little different than his age in 1879 would indicate, it is undoubtedly the correct baptism record since it is the only Janos Almassy born around this period in Nagy Saros. His death record could be sought for additional evidence.

The marriage record says that Susanna Hnath was 35 years old, indicating that she was born about 1844 or 1845. There were two Susanna Hnaths baptized in the Ujak Greek Catholic parish during this time.:

1. Susana, baptized on 11 May 1844, was the daughter of Johannes Hnat and Maria Mihaly (27)

2. Susana baptized August 1845, was the daughter of Andras Hnat and Catharina Oszfrin (28)

Swatches were done in the Ujak Greek Catholic death and marriage records to see if these Susanas could be eliminated. There were no entries for either in the periods in which they would have most likely died as infants , small children ,or unmarried. Interestingly, Anna Hnat, the two-year-old daughter of Andras Hnat, was buried on 2 July 1847 in Ujak. Searches for Anna's birth around 1845 were negative, so it is possible that this child, Anna, was Andras Hnats's daughter Susanna, born in 1845. Anna could be short for Susanna. However, this is uncommon, and additional evidence is needed to prove that Susanna is the ancestor. The best way to do this is to find the ancestral Sussanna (Hnath) Almassy's death record in Nagy Saros. The 1904 marriage of her daughter Rozalia indicated that Sususana was still living at that time and resided in Nagy Saros. She would have been around 60 years old. Her son, Istvan Ludwig Almassy, was married in 1911, and his marriage record indicates that she was still alive then as well. Searches were conducted in the civil record by the civil registration office in Velky Saris. They answered that Suzanna's death wasn't found. It is not known how thoroughly they checked the records or the year span that was checked.

SUMMARY

The objective of this research session was to determine the origins of Andre C. Sinay and Rosalia Almassy and to locate them in the records of that place. This was accomplished. Andrew Charles Sinay was born Andras Szinai on 8 August 1879 in Nagy-Saros, Saros Country, Hungary (now Velky Saris, Slovakia). Roasalia Almassy was born Rozalia Maria Almassy on 28 August 1880 in Kasss, Abauj-Torna County, Hungary (now Kosice, Slovakia.   Andras and Rozalia's parents were identified, as well as several of their grandparents.

Susanna Hnath's parents remain unknown. Until a death record or other evidence of her parents' names can be found, it is not possible to differentiate between the two Susanna Hnaths born in Ujak near the time of her birth.

A SHORT HISTORY OF
JOHN M. LABAK FAMILY

The following is a short history I wrote from the research I received from ancestry.com. The research by ancestry.com is in Appendix B, along with the documents to back up the research of the Labak ancestry. As an introduction to the findings by ancestry. com, I recommend reading my summary here and then reading the research by ancestry.com. After reading both writings, the reader should know what the ancestry people discovered about John Labak.

John Labak, our paternal grandfather, was born on March 13, 1894, in Zilina, Slovakia, to Anna Liko and died in Canton, Ohio, on September 16, 1968. He was born Joannes Liko and came to America on April 17, 1914, as Jan Liko. Grandpa sailed from Bremen, Germany, at 18 and indicated his previous residence as Volenice, Trencsen, Hungary, near Rosina. His destination was Ford City, Pennsylvania. He would spend some time there (fewer than two years) before he arrived in Canton, Ohio. Even though he came as Jan Liko, he indicated his father was Jan Labak and that he was born in Zilina (the Slovakian name of the city), also known in Hungarian as Zsolna. Volenice was where he was living when he departed Slovakia. The verification of his birth in Zilina is correct, yet the shipping record was the actual verification of his personage.

A birth registry does indicate his birth to Anna Liko, indicating he was illegitimate; his godparents were Jan Labak and Susanna (maybe Debreska) of Roszina, a town a short distance south of Zilina. Ochodnicz was where Anna Liko was from, a short distance north of Zilina. Roszina is now Rosina, Slovakia. All of these towns were in the Hungarian empire during the birth of Jan, so they all had Hungarian names. Grandpa still indicated a variety of origins in several forms in the United States. On one, he indicated he was from Austria. On another, he indicated he was from Czechoslovakia. The truth is simply that he was born in Slovakia and spoke Slovak. He indicated on one form that he spoke Czech, but there is no telling if he did speak it. He spoke Slovak to my mother, Ann Labak Sinay. The languages are different but similar enough that someone from that region could speak the language and understand, whereas if he had come from East Slovakia (the origin of my father's mother and father, Slovak would be a bit different—similar to the dialectical differences of English in the United States).

Anna Liko was from Ochodnica, Slovakia. Her father was either Martin or Jozsef Liko, who were brothers. These two individuals married sisters or cousins, and one of the two had a daughter, Anna Liko, who was our grandfather's mother. It would take additional research (and a lot of money) to clarify that determination. I only requested to find the parents of John Labak and Mary Labak. At this point, there are two likely candidates: Anna Liko. One was born on November 19, 1873 (in all likelihood, this is her as today is November 19, 2014, and her birthday!), and the other was born on May 28, 1877, the daughter of Martin Liko and Barbara Platek. The first Anna died on March 8, 1952, but was not listed as married. The second Anna passed away on December 16, 1953, and was married to Anton Lazarek. In either case, one of the two is the mother of Jan Liko, our grandfather. I will not be pursuing additional information on this mystery, as the amount of money spent on this research is all I can attribute to it now. Perhaps in the future, I will continue the search. (It would take an additional 2500 dollars to research the parent's names definitively). At this point, I have learned what is necessary for the cousins, a determination of the origins of both grandparents.

Maria Sabel/Zahumensky Labak was born on September 11, 1894, in Nagytapolcsany, Hungary, now modern-day Topolcany, Slovakia. She arrived in New York on September 11, 1912, at 18. Her destination was Perth Amboy, New Jersey, where she was to join her brother-in-law, Jozsef Kovacsik. We do not know who this is, but this is what the shipping record says, and we think it was just made up. She was listed on the shipping record as Maria Zahumenski, single and 18. She listed her nearest relative as her mother, Magda Zahumenski, who also lived in Nagy Topolcany, Hungary. Magda is a shortened version of Magdalena. Grandma wrote her mother's name on her social security application as Maggie. Roman Catholic baptism records were searched for her, but none were found for Maria Zahumensky, Maria Shabel, Sabel, or Shaba. Grandma did list her maiden name, Sabel, on the birth certificates for all four of her children. This is her mother's maiden name before her mother married Steven Zahumensky, and they then had three additional girls: Veronica, Anna, and Rosalia. Anna and Rosalia were twins. Rosalia married Joseph Zarta and came to Canada in 1934. They had two children: Anna and Gary. Anna still lives in Sarnia, Ontario, in Canada. She is married to James Laroque. I have often spoken with her about what she remembers about the Labak family. She verified that Magdalena Sabel had Mary first illegitimately and then married Stephen Zahumensky or Zahumensky. Grandma came to America with the name Zahumensky, but then she changed to her mother's maiden name, Sabel, when she started filling out forms here, including her marriage certificate.

What I wanted to achieve has been partially completed, but this is all I could get for the money (1,500 dollars) I gave them for this search. I lost my first genealogist to a transfer to another job and then inherited another genealogist who took up the task and dragged his feet for months, giving the excuse that a document had yet to arrive. The document was then not even a part of the equation. He spent a lot of time working on this, but he performed tasks that wasted the time I paid for by searching for the name of Swansigar. That was a name on my father's side of the family. Not sure why he did that. In any case, it has been determined that our grandparents were both born in Slovakia, and both traveled to the United States as very young people and somehow met, perhaps at the Slovak Club in Canton, Ohio. They were married on May 20, 1916, at 21 and 22. It would not be long before they would have four children, and Grandpa Labak had a lot of work to keep them in clothes and fed. He was an extremely hard worker. He ran the grocery store in Southwest Canton at 1655 Stark Avenue for many years. He worked at the steel mill when he first got to Canton, but then saved enough to open a grocery store, which he successfully ran for many years from the 1920s' s through the Great Depression until the 1940s before he passed it on to my parents, who had it for a few years. It has not been determined how Grandma Labak got to Canton, Ohio, but it appears that her father was there from Slovakia and that when she joined him and her mother, she ended up in Canton. Her parents did not stay in Ohio and returned to Slovakia. Neither of her two other sisters, Anna or Veronica, ever came to America to live permanently, but Rosalia did visit them in Slovakia when she was alive. Grandpa and Grandma made separate trips to Slovakia in 1936 and 1938, but we are uncertain who they met. We assume they went to see their parents.

So, the Labaks are ethnically Slovaks, and our nationality is Slovakian. The countrymen today refer to themselves as Slovakians. They speak Slovak, a Slavic language like Russian, Czech, Polish, etc. As a part of this report, I am including the writing done by the genealogist and all of the documents that came along with his report. In the end, he did a credible job. It took forever because I started this in April of this year.

The four children that John and Mary Labak had are as follows, along with their children, so the ancestry can see who everyone is:

1. John Labak and Helen Shryock: Marlene, Suzzanne, Gloria, John, Patty

2. Andy Sinay and Ann Labak: Gary, Rosemary, Diane, Tom, Dick, and Andy.

3. Joe Orzeck and Julie Labak: Kathy, John, Elizabeth, and Joe.

4. Joseph Labak and Helen Hlas: Vicky, Michael, Joe and Helen.

Indeed, it was beautiful to be able to see several of my cousins on my trip across the country: Mike and Laura Labak, Father Joe Labak, Helen Marie Labak Zamanek, Vicky Labak Gusthaus, John Orzeck, Gloria Labak Gewelke, and Tricia Labak Golden, whose passion for the truth of the origins of the Labak family is beyond mine. Thank you all for meeting me and for sharing stories of the history of the Labak side of my family. Please stay in touch. Finally, if anyone finds any of this information erroneous, please email me, and I will update the report more truthfully. At this point, this is what we know.

RESEARCH REPORT FOR JOHN M. LABAK FAMILY

This is the research report from ancestry.com on John M. Labak and Mary Labak's ancestry. This detailed report justifies with complete research on where he and his wife were born, where they married, and when they came to America. It was a painstaking task to rewrite this report, but it was necessary to share it with as many ancestors as possible. When the reader sees a number in parentheses after a sentence, it references a document that will follow this report.

JOHN AND MARY LABAK

JOHN M. LABAK

According to his application for a social security number, John Labak was born on 13 March 1895 in Czechoslovakia. His World War I draft registration card listed his birthday as 13 March 1895 as well, but it also gave the town where he was born: Zilina (written sloppily and where the "i" is not dotted, looking like Zilma instead), Austria. (B1) This is very likely the place known as Zilnia, which is in Slovakia today. Zilnia is a city (formerly known as Zsolnain Nyitra County, Hungary) and one of the eight Slovak administrative regions (i.e., Zilina Kraj).

John's application for a Social Security account number gave his parents' names as John Labak and Susan Dubreska. Searches in the database "Slovakia, Church and Synagogue Books, 1592 to 1910" on *FamilySearch* found people with the surname Labak and Dubreska in the Zilina region. John's baptism record was not found, but not all baptisms have been indexed here.

Civil registration began in the Kingdom of Hungary on 1 October 1895. John was born just a few months too early to have a civil birth record, so his inclusion in original church registers became the source of supplicant searches. The registers over several years were examined in Zilina, which was more densely populated than most areas through Upper Hungary and was, therefore, somewhat time-consuming. Only one plausible candidate was discovered.

Joannes (John) Liko was found to have been the only child on the 13th of March 1895 in Zilina. He was the illegitimate son of Anna Liko of Ochodnicz, Trencsen, Hungary, but a resident of Zsolna (Zilina). While this might initially seem an unlikely stretch of the imagination, the godparents were Johannes Labak and Susanna of Roszina, Trencsen, Hungary. Ochodnicz, now known as Ochodnica, Slovakia, was a short distance north of Zilina. Roszina, now Rosina, Slovakia, is a southern suburb of Zilnia.

Research in the registers of Rosina did not disclose any further references for Joannes Labak and Susanna, thus retaining the mystery of Susanna's surname for comparison against Dubresca. Searches were made in marriage records for the marriages of Johannes (5) and in the birth registers to see if Joannes and Susanna had children of their own christened there, all without success from 1878 to 1898. searches of marriages were also made in Zilnia for the same period (but ending in 1896), to no avail.

It was only when research shifted to passenger lists in the United States again that the answer was further solidified. Arriving through Ellis Island on 17th April 1914, having sailed from Bremen, Germany, was Jan (John/ Joannes) Liko. His previous residence was Volenice, Trencsen, Hungary, near Rosina. Although surnamed Liko, he indicated his nearest living relative was his father, Jan Labak, a resident of Volenice. Furthermore, John Liko indicated he was born in Zsolna/Zilnia. This removed all doubt that the ancestral John Labak was born as Johannes/ Jan Liko.

There were two likely candidates for Anna Liko in Ochodnica. One was born on 19th November 1873, the daughter of Jozsef Liko and Anna Platek. There was a notation next to her name that she died on the 8th of March 1952, but no notation of a marriage. The second Anna was born on the 28th of May 1877, the daughter of Martin Liko and Barbara Platek. She was noted as passing away on the 16th of December 1953 and was married to Anton Lazarek.

While Martin was listed as 40 years old on his marriage record in 1871, there were no such individuals born in the area in 1831. However, if he was errantly listed as 40 instead of 30, the only

Martin Liko born in that area was a brother of Jozsef Liko. Jozsef was aged 20 at the time of his marriage in 1866. Jozsef's birth was discovered on 9 March 1846, the son of Joannes Liko and Anna Polacsek. Martin was born on 28 August 1842, the son of the same parents. And was the only Martin born in Ochodnica, or former Trencsen County, between 1825 and 1851. If this Martin represents the man who married Barbara Platek, then it likely means that brothers married sisters(or cousins). However, the Platek spouses could not be defined explicitly in Ochodnica yet. Joseph were indeed brothers, and the lineage links back to their parents, regardless of which was the father of the ancestral Anna.

Further research should be able to discern these individuals further, and if Martin and Jozef were indeed brothers, then the lineage links back to their parents, regardless of which was the gathering of the ancestral Anna. Additional research should also discern the location referred to for the Labaks–John's last resident before immigrating to the United States. Once identified with greater detail, the Labaks can be better segregated and identified in earlier registers and traced back in time.

MARIA (ZAHUMENSKY) LABAK

John's wife was named Mary. One family story says that Mary was illegitimate and took the name Sable, which was her mother's maiden name. Mary's application for a Social Security account number was ordered, knowing it would give her parent's name and a birthday. According to this record, dated 23 January 1952 and filled out by Mary herself, Mary Labak's maiden name was Mary Zahuminski. She was born on the 11th of September 1894 in Czechoslovakia. Her father was Steve Zahumensky, and her mother was Maggie Sable. An entry for John and Mary's marriage was located in an index to Stark County, Ohio marriages. They married on the 20th of May 1916 in Stark County, Ohio. The entry indicates that John Labak married Mary Sable.

The 1920 and 1930 censuses show that Mary immigrated in 1912. Her passenger list was found once her maiden name Zahumenski was determined. This passenger list shows that she arrived in New York on the 11th of September 1912. She was listed as Mary Zahumenski, 18 years old and single. Her nationality was listed as Hungarian, while her race was listed as Slovak. Her last residence and birthplace was Nagytapolcsany, Hungary. This is the Nagy Topolcany found in former Nitro County, Hungary, Now Toby Connie Slovakia. Maria's nearest European relative was her mother, Magda Zahuminski, who lived in Napa County. Magda is the Hungarian and shortened version of Magdalena or, as Mary wrote in her application for a social security number, Maggie. Maria's destination was Perth Amboy, New Jersey, and she was joining her brother-in-law, Joseph Catholic of 296 Street in Perth Amboy, New Jersey.

Roman Catholic baptism records for Nagy Topolcany are available at the family history library. These records were searched from 1893 to 1895 for the baptism of Maria Zahumensky or Sable. Strangely, it still needs to be found. There were no baptism entries for anyone with either of those surnames or any close variation.

SUMMARY

Despite the challenges and the waiting time for some of the sources utilized, this session has undoubtedly discovered the mystery behind John Labak and his origins. Johannes and John Labak were likely to serve as a godparent as his biological parent's father based on the fact that he called him father when he emigrated. Research on 20th-century Parish civil records in Slovakia will likely be needed to link the family to before 1895. However, once that correspondence arrives, research should move expeditiously through the earlier records in Salt Lake City. Lilac lineage may require the same to distinguish which Anna was the ancestor, but it is almost certain that they all converge in earlier generations.

Remaining is the challenge for the Zahumensky lineage. Like the Labak line, some concerted effort will uncover the answers to this pedigree portion. Writing to the parish or Civil Authorities in Nagy Topolcany should uncover more for Maria and her mother, Magdalena. They lived there later in life, but Maria was born elsewhere before they moved there. Continued patience and persistence will be the keys to solving the challenges for all branches. With this in mind, continued research is highly recommended. For anyone who wishes to view the tree I created, please send me your email address and I will send you a link for you to have access to the tree.

AUTHOR BIOGRAPHY

Richard Sinay was a high school and college English and reading teacher for schools in Orange County, California, for thirty-seven years. Recently, he has been writing books about his past and teaching career. He has written two previous books: *Who We Met on the Way to Stanford: A Father's Memoir* and *How to Get a Golf Scholarship to Stanford: A Parent's Guide*. He spends part of his time playing golf and reading and writing. He is working on a series of books about his experiences in education in California. He resides in Palm Desert, California, with his wife, Tina.

INDEX OF 2014 USA TRIP: CITIES AND SITES VISITED

Phoenix, AZ: I met a high school friend and his wife, a Facebook friend, and we had a great lunch and talked about all things La Habra High School and Politics and Religion.

Denver, CO: I met my cousin Monica Sinay Turner and her husband. I had a wonderful stay with them overnight, a great conversation about family, and a great dinner.

Charleston, SC: I met a cousin, Mike Labak, and his wife for lunch. It was great to see someone I had not seen for fifty years.

Albuquerque, NM: I met my first cousin, Carol-Sinay L'Esperance, at their house, went to lunch, and they went to Old Town Albuquerque and stayed overnight.

St. Augustine, FL: I visited one of the oldest cities in the country and realized the Spanish were in control of a part of our country for some time in our history. The city reflects that beginning.
Augusta, GA: I had an extraordinary time meeting Mark Ritchie and his friend Pat at Sheehan's Irish Pub. Both had just played Augusta National and talked about their round when I overheard the conversation. I joined them for a drink and promptly hit it off

with them. We got drunk, and they invited me to play Augusta Country Club the next day.

<u>New Orleans, LA:</u> New Orleans was both delightful and disappointing. I love the food and the atmosphere, but the annoying beggars make the experience less enjoyable. The music and the culture are fascinating, and the city does grow on one after some time.

<u>Ft. Lauderdale, FL</u> This was not a city I explored, but it is where my cousin Terry Hull lived. We had a wonderful time over Chinese food and talked about many subjects, including family.

<u>Nashville, TN:</u> What is not to like about musicland? There are so many young artists trying to make it to the top. It would have been fun to see young Taylor Swift working her way up the ladder of the music world. I loved the town except for the cost of the parking!

<u>Denver, CO:</u> Denver is a little big town with many restaurants and oil companies. I like the people for the most part, but it was my cousin Monica David that I thoroughly enjoyed with her husband.

<u>Savannah, GA:</u> Savannah was one of the best cities I visited on this trip because it was so well organized. That was due to the work by James Oglethorpe, the urban designer way before this time.

<u>Columbus, OH:</u> Columbus is the home of Ohio State University and the premier college of Ohio, although it could be a better part of the town. I am glad I went to an Orange County college instead of that university.

<u>Canton, OH:</u> Canton is where I was born, and many of my cousins still live. I loved visiting the old neighborhood where I grew up

and saw the deterioration sixty years later. The city of Canton looks good, but the old neighborhood shows the poverty of the Southwest of Canton.

Woodstock, Ill: How would I not know that this is the town where they filmed Groundhogs Day, the hilarious movie of the guy who lives the same day over and over? It is a classic movie, and seeing the town square that Bill Murry walked through was just special.

Lake Oswego, CA: The town of my cousin Doug Sinay, who I met where he worked and spent half a day with him. The Bill Sinay family were the first people we were with when we got to California. It was great seeing Doug and sharing old memories.

Cannonsburg, PA: This is my grandfather's home and the place of my father's birth. It was a dilapidated town because it was a steel mill that had its heyday. It was now an old and poverty-stricken town, the way of all manufacturing in this country.

Hannibal, MO: The home of Mark Twain and one of the highlights of my trip. Seeing where this genius was born is a testimony to the power of reading. Twain read his way out of poverty and became one of the most celebrated authors in American Literature.

Medford, OR: This is where I met my cousin Patti Labak Golden and spent the day and night talking about family and ancestry. It was an enlightening session and one filled with more questions than answers.

Bethlehem, PA: The home of Bethlehem Steel, the biggest steel manufacturer in the country at the height of its day.

Napa, CA: Napa is a fun place to go if one is into wine. There are so many wine places to visit and enjoy. I spent a good deal of time trying to find the magic elixir.

Detroit, MI: Detroit was under remediation, looking better than the run-down city I had seen several years earlier. It is not my favorite town, and I imagine there were better times for it.

Seattle, WA: My daughter, her husband, and granddaughter's home. We had a wonderful time when I was there, and it was special.

San Francisco, CA: Are you going to San Francisco, where the hippie revolution occurred in the 60s? It is an incredible city to visit and one of my favorite cities in the country.

Los Gatos, CA: This is a neat little town where my son, his wife, and my two grandchildren live. We had a wonderful time playing baseball and doing all sorts of fun things.

Grass Valley, CA: this was where I met my cousin Debra Sinay Willis and had a spectacular time going around town, drinking wine, and eating good food. It was a special time to discuss family and the good and the bad of being a product of our parent's parenting.

Sedona, AZ: What a beautiful place of art and architectural beauty. I did not spend enough time in Sedona, but the little I did told me that it is a great place to live.

Harbor Town, SC: Harbor Town was the home of the Harbor Town Links, where an important PGA tournament is played each year, with the winner wearing a plaid jacket. It was an incredible course to play, and I thoroughly enjoyed it.

<u>Bloomfield Hills, MI:</u> Bloomfield is the home of Oakland Hills Country Club. I was so fortunate to play these courses that are important to the history of golf. Major championships are played there like six US Opens and three PGA championships. It is a venue where anyone would want to win major championships.

<u>Yellowstone, WY:</u> Yellowstone National Park is one of the great wonders of our country, and being able to see Old Faithful, a geyser that goes off regularly, is one of the great joys of living in America.

<u>Grand Canyon, AZ:</u> How can anyone not enjoy the magnificent beauty of the Grand Canyon in Arizona? What an incredible spectacle and what a joy it was to stand near the edge and look over into the abyss. This is not for the faint-hearted, and I thought people tip-toe on the edges are just exercising a death wish.

<u>Sonoma, CA:</u> Another wine country, beautiful and fun city to visit. I went there just after the earthquake, and the town will need a lot of repairs. I visited a high school with a Facebook friend, Catherine Clemens Sevenau. We had a wonderful day together.

<u>Mount Rushmore, SD:</u> It is one of the tremendous artistic feats of the century and amazing to see. I just did not take the trip to get a closer look at the accomplishment, but what I saw was just unbelievable.

<u>Williamsburg, VA:</u> Visiting the 18th-century historical town was fantastic. I enjoyed the history and the atmosphere created by this beautiful historical society.

<u>West Hampton, NY:</u> Going to the Hamptons is quite a treat; there, one will find people of many means. Fortunately, it was visiting my cousin Gloria Labak Gewelke and her husband, Don. We had

a wonderful time with them and found the ancestry conversation fascinating, and learning about their lives and family was just as enjoyable.

<u>Nevada City, CA:</u> Another place where Mark Twain hung out and another place my cousin Debra Sinay Willis went to for fun.

<u>Prospect, OR:</u> Perhaps the most interesting cousin of all, John Orzeck, whose mother was my mother's sister, Julie Labak Orzeck. I spent time with John and his wonderful lady friend. We ate Chinese food and talked about the family and the history of the family. It was pretty interesting.

<u>Issaquah, WA:</u> This is where my daughter Jennie was teaching during my visit. Her husband, Matt, works in the same town for the SanMar Corporation.

<u>Rancho Bernardo, CA:</u> This is a lovely town next to where I lived during my trip in Escondido, CA.

<u>Baltimore, MD:</u> The town where Edgar Alan Poe is laid to rest and where he was last seen before his untimely death.

<u>Philadelphia, PA:</u> The City of Brotherly Love and the town where the Constitution was written and the Liberty Bell resides. It has a long history and is a great food place to enjoy.

<u>Taos, NM:</u> The town is like a cartoon because the houses in their Pueblo style are a delight. The art created in this city is some of the best in the country.

GOLF COURSES PLAYED

Louisiana TPC: The Home of the Zurich Classic

The TPC Players Club: The Home of the Players Championship
Harbor Town Golf Links: The Home of the RBC Heritage

Augusta Country Club: The Sister Country Club to Augusta
National Golf Course

Oakland Hills CC North and Oakland Hills CC South: The South
Course is the home of many major championships.

Bull Valley CC: Home course of Mark Ritchie just outside of
Woodstock, Illinois. We had a wonderful day playing golf at this
course.

Golden Horseshoe Course: Williamsburg, VA

Bandon Dunes and Pacific Dunes, Bandon, Oregon

Pebble Beach, Spyglass Hill, and Spanish Bay in Pebble Beach,
California

NATIONAL PARKS VISITED

Grand Canyon National Park

Yellowstone National Park

Mount Rushmore National Park

FAMOUS SITES VISITED

Football Hall of Fame in Canton, OH

The McKinley Library and Museum, Canton, OH

World Golf Hall of Fame in St. Augustine, FL

Disney World in Orlando, FL

Henry Ford Museum, Dearborn, MI

San Francisco Wharf, San Francisco, CA

Old Faithful at Yellowstone National Park, Yellowstone, WY

Edgar Alan Poe Gravesite, Saloon, Restaurant, and Museum, Baltimore, MD

Independence Hall, Philadelphia, PA

Liberty Bell, Philadelphia, PA

Hotel Monteleone, New Orleans, LA